CONQUERING THE

GENERATIONAL CHALLENGE

CREATING A HARMONIOUS AND PRODUCTIVE WORKPLACE

CONQUERING THE

GENERATIONAL CHALLENGE

CREATING A HARMONIOUS AND PRODUCTIVE WORKPLACE

DAVID A. BUTLER
KEITH A. NEUBER

First Edition

ISBN 978-0-578-57065-5

Contents

Foreword

This book is the work of two people who share a common interest: they find how people interact in the workplace fascinating. As we all know, when people work together, it can be either harmonious or chaotic. The aim of this book—and the passion and purpose of the authors—is to help you achieve the former. While Keith Neuber and David Butler agree on the goal, they provide very different commentary on the challenges, particularly the generational challenges, in the workplace. David, a business leader, comes with an immense background of real experiences that help him create stories that bring these challenges to life. Keith, a psychologist, provides in-depth commentary on why we do the things we do and how we can change for the better. They create the yin-yang of understanding both the challenge and the solution.

The concept was born in the trenches of the business world. Years of experiencing communication challenges among all generations showed them the need to provide tools so that generations could better understand each other. Its infancy happened over five-plus years of researching and studying the challenge and what successful companies had done to overcome it. Countless hours were spent with Gartner (formerly CEB) asking questions and pouring over data they had accumulated. The concept's childhood was comprised of studying myriads of data capture and surveys[1], interviewing countless people of all generations to get their experiential input, and seeking real-life examples of generational dysfunction in the workplace. It became an adult when David and Keith started having conversations about the challenge and solutions to overcome it. What better way to learn than through stories? Now, as this concept enters the business world, it has years of knowledge and wisdom in its wake, and it's ready to be shared with people of all generations to help make business culture more harmonious and productive. As you read through the stories in this book and understand Keith and David's message, the hope is that you will be able to easily gain perspective and learn how to create a workplace where everyone can do their best.

---

[1] There are many research works available for study. Included in these are works from Gartner, Deloitte, SHRM and a multitude of private companies who focus on this subject matter.

Acknowledgments

David:

First and foremost, I would like to thank my wonderful wife Sara for not only supporting me through this effort, but encouraging me every step of the way. "You're THE BEST"! I would also like to thank my mentor Jaede for stimulating me to become interested in this subject matter many years ago. You taught me the key lesson of "make it simple for me". Lastly, and most importantly, I would like to thank my Lord and Savior Jesus Christ for giving me the blessing of this book and countless other "rams" throughout my life.

Keith:

I would like to thank my wife Paula for her love and support through the years of my chasing windmills. I would also like to thank my son Patrick for his insights and encouragement in my quest to make a difference.

Both:

We would like to thank everyone, from all generations, who shared pieces of their lives in order to make the stories come to life. Your generational dysfunction situations have become valuable to others. We would also like to thank everyone who did a "first read" on the original manuscript and provided the feedback required to make it better.

We would like to thank Preston Cannon of Ramsey Press for providing guidance and introducing us to the best literary production team available . . . Jennifer Gingerich (editor), Micah Kandros (external designer), and Mandi Cofer (internal designer). You have taken our labor and turned it into something special.

Introduction: David

As a card-carrying baby boomer (oh yeah, that card is a membership in AARP!), I feel like I grew up in the most wonderful, most exciting time ever. OK, I admit that every generation probably feels that same way; each for their own reasons. As a boomer, I got to experience firsthand some of the most important events in history; the J.F.K. assassination, Martin Luther King Jr., man landing on the moon, the British invasion (you boomers will know what that is), the creation of the computer, and the revolution for social equality. It was a time of community picnics and families watching television together on Saturday night—not to mention *Saturday Night Live*. Being social meant going downtown on Friday nights to greet friends, and in later years, going to the mall. Being part of a group meant getting together in someone's backyard for a corn roast. I remember all too well spending hours in the public library scouring through Encyclopedia Britannica to research a term paper.

I have also witnessed many changes in the business world. I remember when there were Sunday "blue laws," "banker's hours," and when

1

there were actually personal sales professionals instead of online shopping. The world has changed. That is a good thing. We have made huge leaps in medical knowledge, information transfer, and modern conveniences. Practically anything you want to know can be available within seconds on the internet. This rapid change in technology however doesn't come without pain. As we have access to more information, we are trending away from personal interactions. This is becoming more evident in the workplace. Who each of us are today is a product of everything we have experienced up until today. And each generation sees the world based on their experiences. People are staying engaged in the workplace for longer, which is creating an environment where four to five generations are working side by side. The purpose of this book is to help you get a better understanding of how each generation thinks and why they think and behave the way they do. Through that understanding you will gain a new insight into how to create a new business workplace where everyone, from all generations, can do their best. Understanding the past and how it influences the present will pave the way for what we need to know about the future workplace.

Let me give you an example.

This is a picture of my mom and dad on their wedding day in 1946. My dad was just a few months shy of his twenty-first birthday. He had just returned from flying twenty-seven missions over Europe in a B-17 bomber. They were a part of the traditionalist generation. His vision of success in life was to work, have a family, buy a house, take a family vacation once a year, and retire at sixty-two years old to a life of relaxation. When he came home from the war, he took advantage of the G.I. Bill and became a journeyman electrician in the International Brotherhood of Electrical Workers. He was an electrician all of his life, never giving any thought to doing anything else. That's what you did professionally in those days.

Years later, this goofy looking baby boomer came along. My vision of success was, initially, to work in a career that was fulfilling, buy a big house, drive a European sports car, and retire early to a life of travel and adventure. I knew what I wanted to do professionally, got the required education, and went to work in that industry. After about nine years, I got bored  with that work and decided to reinvent my career. As a boomer, I wanted to explore beyond traditional channels. Boomers were always interested in what else might be out there. When I told my dad (the traditionalist) what I intended to do, he looked at me like I had two heads. He didn't have the capacity to comprehend why someone would want to do such a thing.

More years later, this wonderful young lady was born. She is a part of the millennial generation. Her vision of success is to balance her family and professional career and have the ability to manage that freely, continue to learn and grow, and be a part of things that add value to society. The picture above is how she likes to work. Education is important to her generation, so is working in a flexible workplace. Sometimes  I find it hard to understand why she doesn't want to go to an office and be part of a face-to-face work team. I guess now I know how my dad felt.

None of us were right; none of us were wrong. We merely formed our perceptions based on the influences and experiences to which we were subjected. Our behaviors followed suit. The point here is that until we start to break down our own biases about generations in the workplace and learn to look at what *can be* instead of how we think things *should be*, we will continue to experience ongoing frustrations. That's what this book is all about—learning to rethink what we have always believed about others in the workplace and reframe a new workplace that makes our businesses more harmonious, collaborative, and productive.

It needs to be noted, however, that generations are not defined merely by years of birth. The years associated with each generation are general guidelines for reference. Generations are more closely defined by significant events as well as years. Take for example our newest upcoming generation, Generation Z (~1998–2015). The people born into this generation only know September 11, 2001, as something they have heard about, seen videos of online, or learned about in their history lessons. They were too young to remember any of the events of that day first-hand. The delineating marker between the millennial generation and Generation Z is personal awareness of that defining moment.

Likewise, just because someone was born into a generation doesn't mean that they automatically assume all of the characteristics associated with it. A major part of developing character and personality comes from parental (and other authority figure) influence. Each of us has experienced different family and social values as well as cultures as we went through our formative years. The characteristics we speak about in this book are generalities associated with people of each generation. The models have been created through extensive surveying and interviewing of people from each generation. Our hope is that, as you read, you will see transparency in yourself and others as you learn why each generation thinks and acts the way they do. Hopefully, you will also learn new things about each generation that help you understand how these characteristics and behaviors were formed. That's part of what makes it fun! We hope you enjoy the experience.

Introduction: Keith

Like David, I was raised in the boomer generation. I grew up in a blue-collar family where my sister and I had all of our daily needs met. My father was a traditionalist. He worked for IBM as a tool maker. He always arrived early for work, where he would read the newspaper while waiting to clock in on time. My father expressed considerable resentment toward the new college graduates who worked at IBM for what he perceived as their lax work ethic. He was a perfectionist, and this strained our relationship because it seemed I was never able to meet his expectations. He would come home from work and walk the yard, digging up dandelions with his pocket knife. I thought he was crazy. But one thing my dad taught me was to work hard. I got my first job as a bellhop on my sixteenth birthday working for Twentieth Century Fox during the making of the movie *Hello, Dolly!* Since then I have always had at least one full- or part-time job. (I currently have three.)

I received good grades in school and became the first person from my father's side of the family to graduate college. During my early years in college I became idealistic and rebellious which strained my relationship even more with my ultra-conservative father. I had entered college as a math major since math had been my strong suit in high school. Unfortunately, I received D's in my first three math classes, became disillusioned, joined a fraternity, and got drunk for a year. I confided in one of my fraternity brothers, Henry Sibly, who told me that everyone who flunked out as a math major became a psychology major. The next day I changed my major to Psychology. I was fortunate to have a young psychology professor, Jeffrey Goldblum, turn me on to research where I could make use of my analytic skills. Well, I got myself turned around, found my calling as a therapist in graduate school at Eastern Kentucky University, and spent the next forty-five years developing my skills at facilitating change through understanding human dynamics.

I have made numerous mistakes in my life and have had enough struggles and life experience to develop an appreciation for different perspectives. I also have a family made up of every generation that comes after my own. I have three generation Xer children (although two seem more like boomers), two millennial grandchildren, two Generation Z grandchildren, and one grandchild from a generation yet to be labeled. What I have to offer this adventure is some theoretical consideration based on human dynamics, including an emphasis on the development of personality traits. I will provide material from two theorists: Erik Erikson and Abraham Maslow. Erikson's Epigenetic Principle focuses on a logical progression of personality development while Maslow's Hierarchy of Needs provides insight into human motivation. Don't worry! I promise not to scare you off. I will provide detail pertaining to the theories in a later chapter, and I'll try not to bore you. As we examine the generations in the following chapters, I will focus on several characteristics that play a significant role in the workplace including self-control, personal boundaries, belongingness needs and self-esteem. I hope that this knowledge and information will give you greater insight into how people become who they are, what makes them tick, and why they behave the way they do. It's going to be a fun ride.

P.S. On any given spring day, you can find me with a screwdriver digging dandelions out of my yard.

PART ONE

Generational Influences: "Why We Are Who We Are"

A millennial was talking to a Generation Xer.

"I feel sorry for you. When you were growing up, you didn't have any of the great things we have today . . . smartphones, Wi-Fi, 5G, Snapchat, Siri and Alexa, YouTube, or Google. How did you even survive?"

The Gen Xer looked at the millennial and said, "You're right. We didn't have any of those things, so we invented them."

CHAPTER ONE

Walter, the Traditionalist

Walter Robertson was born on a sweltering July morning in 1925. His mother, Elizabeth, was comfortable in her hospital room with fresh air blowing into the room from the window fan. Elizabeth cherished the baby boy she held in her arms, but at the same time she was anxious about having another child for which to provide. Her husband, Samuel, rented a meager farm in rural Virginia. They were able to produce most of the staple foods they needed to survive, but not much more. She knew from experience that children needed a lot of things that cost money, and they didn't have much of that. Deep inside she believed that they would make it somehow, and she began thinking of ways she could earn a little extra money to help out. Mrs. Swanson up the lane might need some help canning in the fall, or maybe Francis Maxwell in the ladies' mission group down at the church knew of someone who needed help cleaning their house.

After the standard five-day hospital stay, Elizabeth took Walter home to meet his five-year-old brother Edwin and his nearly-four-year-old sister Lois. Lois was given the task of helping out with the baby. Harvest time was fast approaching, and Edwin would continue to help his father in the fields. There wasn't an extra room in the small farmhouse, so Elizabeth made a comfortable little pallet on the floor next to her bed for Walter. Tears of worry filled her eyes, but in her heart, she knew they would be OK. Yet, the rain stopped for the season and the crops withered in the field. By October it was clear that the family could no longer stay at the only place the children had ever known as home. They packed up the few belongings they had and traveled to Lynchburg so Samuel could look for work. Samuel was a hardworking man who had learned many skills out of necessity. He was fortunate to find work as a helper in a small carpentry shop, and because he was a quick learner, he soon mastered the trade. For now, it seemed that they would be alright.

In September of 1929, when Walter was just four years old, the country plunged into a deep depression. Samuel's work was nearly eliminated. He was able to pick up odd jobs repairing houses that began to crumble, and he learned to make basic furniture to sell to those who couldn't afford to buy from the few retail stores that remained. Edwin and Walter also started looking for small ways to make a little money, spending long hours doing whatever they could to earn just a few pennies. Edwin walked to a farm outside of town to help pick and shuck corn to feed the few cattle the farmer had left; Walter swept floors in a few of the shops in town. Their family was one of the more fortunate ones. Most families lost everything and spent their days in soup lines to keep their stomachs from grumbling. Walter's family learned how to do whatever was required to survive. They saved every penny and constantly looked for ways to cut costs.

Two months after Walter's sixth birthday, his mother gave birth to a baby girl. The hospital rules stated that children under the age of twelve were not allowed inside the hospital, especially in the maternity ward. So Walter and his siblings didn't get to meet their baby sister until she came home five days later. Elizabeth had always been an avid reader and spent hours reading to her children. Their favorite stories were about the Trojan War and Odysseus's long journey home. So when the kids met their bright-eyed new sister, they urged Elizabeth to name her Helen after the famous Helen of Troy. Samuel smiled in agreement as he stared with wonder at his growing family.

Then in 1932, the telltale signs of a problem began when little Helen developed a severe cold. Elizabeth took her to the local doctor who told her how to help get her baby well again. Elizabeth tended to Helen constantly, but the notorious coughing began two weeks later. The next weeks were agony as Helen struggled for breath. The children didn't know how to help. They openly cried for their beloved little sister. Samuel cried on the inside, trying desperately to be strong for his family.

The house fell silent four weeks later when little Helen passed away. Elizabeth fell into a deep depression. Lois refused to leave her mother's side. Even though Samuel's own heart was broken, he tried to remain strong. He took Edwin and Walter aside and tried to explain. He told them that a man's loyalty was always due to those around him—God first, family second, and job third. He went on to say that a man is measured by how he reacts in hard times. He said there would be times in life when they would need to make tough decisions and to remember that a real man never forgets his loyalty. Years later, Walter would be offered a position that would require him to relocate his own family overseas. It was a huge opportunity, but one that would be hard on his wife and children. Walter remembered his father's words about loyalty and politely declined the opportunity for the sake of his family.

As the world continued to struggle economically, new faces appeared on the political scene. In January 1933, German President Paul Von Hindenburg appointed a rising young organizer named Adolph Hitler as chancellor of that country. Hitler's meteoric rise to power in the German government was marked by intolerance, violence, and aggression. On September 1, 1939, Hitler invaded Poland to extend the philosophy of the superiority of the Arian Nation. This level of hate and oppression to others, simply because he saw them as obstacles to his system of dominance, was beginning to threaten the world. The situation had escalated beyond tolerance and on September 3 the United Kingdom and France declared war on Germany.

Samuel's family gathered around the little radio they had in their parlor and listened as the news unfolded of this new war. Samuel and Elizabeth were terrified, having recently lived through World War I. They were concerned for Lois who had recently married and was beginning her own family. Eighteen-year-old Edwin and fourteen-year-old Walter listened with bated breath. This was the biggest and most exciting thing they had ever heard. On December 7, 1941, Japan raided the United States naval base at Pearl Harbor, Hawaii. Within days, the United States entered the war.

Walter was extremely jealous of his brother Edwin, who at eighteen soon joined the war effort. It seemed to Walter that every young man was anxious to teach the Axis powers a lesson. Because Walter still wasn't old enough to enlist, he had no choice but to watch all the other young men in Lynchburg march off to glory. Walter waited and watched, and on his eighteenth birthday in 1943, he enlisted in the Army Air Corp. Elizabeth cried as her second son boarded the bus to become a soldier. Following basic training, Walter was sent to gunnery school in Kingman, Arizona—a time of great excitement for him. The army experience was the first time he had ever been outside of the state of Virginia. He worked hard and listened to everything his sergeant told him and was soon promoted to corporal. He learned that doing not only what was expected but looking for ways to be the best led to great rewards. Walter was a good soldier and rose through the ranks. By the time he was honorably discharged in 1945, he had attained the rank of staff sergeant.

So far in life, Walter had learned frugality; that hard work pays off, that a strong family unit can accomplish most anything together, and that playing by the rules gets you ahead. But now that he was a civilian once again, he wondered what lay beyond. Back home in Virginia, Walter started to look at his options. In 1944, President Roosevelt signed the Servicemen's Readjustment Act. Also known as the G.I. Bill, this program allowed returning servicemen to receive tuition to complete high school, attend college, or attend a vocational or technical school. When Walter learned of this, he immediately began looking for the educational opportunity that was right for him. He had learned that education and working smart led to much bigger things than farming and job-hopping. He soon discovered Virginia A&M in Blacksburg, Virginia, applied, and was accepted. Walter moved to Blacksburg for the fall semester in 1945, enrolling in the School of Engineering. He rented a room in a boardinghouse in order to save money and worked nights and weekends at the local movie theater to help make ends meet. He studied diligently and applied all of the life lessons he had learned while in the army. Samuel smiled with pride and Elizabeth had tears in her eyes on that spring day in 1949 when they watched the first person in their family graduate from college.

Soon thereafter, Walter began his career as a mechanical engineer with a small firm in Charlottesville, Virginia. He was dedicated to his work and within two years was rewarded with a promotion. The firm was expanding into the Richmond market and Walter was asked to open the new office. He readily accepted the position and relocated to the Midlothian area in October of 1951. He now had five other men working in his new organization. He also had a secretary, Martha Edgewater. He was thankful that her shorthand, filing, and typing skills were immaculate. Having her there to handle all of his administrative work allowed him to manage the other employees more effectively.

Walter laid out the rules of how the office would be run. Each man would be paid $3,300 per year, a good wage for the work they would be expected to perform. Martha worked for considerably less. Business hours were from 8:00 a.m. until 5:00 p.m. Monday through Friday, with a thirty-minute lunch break. Each of them was expected to be in the office every day. A suit and tie were the only acceptable attire, and their white shirts were expected to be starched and ironed. Dress hats were optional. After their second year of employment, the men would earn a week of paid vacation. If they wished to use it, they must submit a request in writing no less than ninety days prior to the requested time-off date. If they were unable to reach any deadlines, they would be expected to work whatever hours were necessary to reach their goals. Smoking at their desk was permitted as long as they kept their ashtrays clean. Walter's team appreciated the leadership he provided. There was a comfortable comradery and even though they referred to him as Mr. Robertson when clients were around, he was just Walt to them whenever they chatted as a team. They worked hard and soon grew the office into one of the most profitable in the organization. Walt rewarded them with a new coffee percolator and a small Kelvinator refrigerator. Martha made sure that there was a fresh pot brewed each morning before they arrived. Life was good for Walt, and he wanted it to stay that way. Walt stood firm on the business beliefs that had made him successful, and his life experiences had taught him the values that led to that success. The business world of his day was consistent, and change was slow, yet it seemed to work for everyone. People were loyal, and they expected their company to be there for them throughout their working years. Walt's business was no different. He continued to lead his company the same way throughout his career. Eventually he realized that he should spend more time enjoying his later years, and he began to relinquish control to others. When that day came, Walt was proud of all he had accomplished.

What shaped the traditionalist generation (aka the builders, the silent generation, and the war generation):

- Stock market crash/the Great Depression
- Roosevelt's New Deal
- Raised by conservative parents
- Hard times followed by prosperity
- Political transformation in Europe/Adolph Hitler/World War II/Pearl Harbor
- Intense nationalism

- Radio
- The Dust Bowl
- Founding of the United Nations
- Polaroid camera
- Korean War
- NATO established

Framework of the workplace as they entered the job market:

- Made up of mostly men
- Large number of veterans (used to taking and giving orders)
- Single-family wage earners (high financial accountability)
- Traditional home/family roles transferred to work
- Advent of technology (automobiles, aircraft, communication)
- Opportunities created by the New Deal and the G.I. Bill
- Face-to-face or telephone communication
- U.S. Postal Service was the single outside communication tool
- Organized work space/offices have value

Work ethic and values:

- Adhere to rules
- Work before play
- Honor commitments and expect accountability
- Value dedication, sacrifice, hard work, and compliance
- Linear work style
- Like hierarchal work environment/top-down management
- Value long-term career
- Want security and stability
- Clearly defined rules/policies
- Value command and control
- Believe that advancement is based on seniority

SO . . . WHAT DOES ALL THIS MEAN?

Walter grew up in a family whose focus was to survive day to day. Hard work was the expectation even when the result was disappointment. Effort was the only variable that individuals could control. Children were expected to help support the family at early ages, whether working in the fields and looking for other opportunities to earn pennies. At this time, a little was perceived as significant. Meeting basic needs was at the core of decision-making for most people. Taking risks like relocating without assurance of enhancement was commonplace. World wars and the Great Depression accentuated vulnerability of both individuals and country.

This time period placed emphasis on the basic elements of life. The early stages of life were ordered with expectations of compliance with parents who were the primary authority figures. As children aged, they were expected to be productive and industrious. It is clear from Walter's story that loyalty was important and expected—God first, family second, work third. After the Great Depression, hard work and determination began to ease the pressures that families had previously experienced in trying to meet basic needs. Parents began to focus on making sure that their children would never have to go through what they had experienced. The creation of jobs shifted mind-sets from survival to security. Threats of war spurred a sense of nationalism, and children and young adults began to identify with the cause of protecting liberty and freedom. Women entered the workforce in previously unfamiliar roles. Traditional marriage was a generally accepted expectation. Veterans and those who worked behind the scenes were perceived as heroes. Innovation became an important bi-product of a dedicated work force that was leading to advances in technology and industrial development. Employees experienced a sense of pride in a job well done.

CHAPTER 2

Nancy, the Baby Boomer

New Year's Eve 1953 was a spectacular night in Richmond, Virginia. The party at John Sinclair's home was an event to be remembered. The weather was unseasonable warm, and guests danced on the veranda until late into the night. Caviar and champagne were the order of the day. The success Walt had achieved as he branched out and started his own engineering firm allowed him to easily be accepted into upper-middle-class society. He and his wife Katherine moved from room to room meeting new friends and reconnecting with old ones.

The ride home was almost as beautiful as the evening. Katherine sat close to Walt as he cruised along in his Buick Skylark convertible.

"What a wonderful night," she whispered to him.

"Yes. Indeed it was," he replied.

She went on, "I think I can make it even better."

"Oh, come now," he shot back. "I really don't think that is possible."

"It is, Walt. I have some wonderful news. We are going to have another baby".

Walt hit the brakes and pulled to the side of the road. He hugged Katherine tight to him and said, "I love you, my darling. And, yes, you have made the night even better."

Nancy Robertson was born on the ninth day of August in 1954. From the start, she was the apple of her daddy's eye. She was a beautiful baby. Except for a few bouts with colic, she was the happiest and easiest baby. Her two older brothers, John and Michael, also adored her. John was four, and Michael was nearly nine. The family lived in a brick ranch in the suburb of Mechanicsville, Virginia, where Nancy and her brothers would later attend Mechanicsville Elementary School. Walt was a typical father of his day, believing in a firm hand with raising the children. Katherine was an advocate of new concepts of child rearing and was heavily influenced by Dr. Benjamin Spock's book *Baby and Child Care*. Where Walt wanted to teach and discipline the children based on his own life experiences, Katherine favored Dr. Spock's concept of treating each of them as individuals. She favored being more flexible and affectionate with them— not forcing them to meet traditional standards. Nancy loved her mother's approach. At the time, she had no idea how this would influence her later in life with her own children.

Life was idyllic for the family in the late 1950s and early '60s. Walt and Katherine provided a secure home and made sure the kids had everything they needed. Nancy and her friends would play in the neighborhood during the summer until the streetlights came on and all of the moms would call their children in. Nancy loved being a "girly-girl," wearing frilly dresses, playing with Barbie dolls with her girlfriends, and helping Katherine in the kitchen. She was, however, without a doubt a "daddy's girl." Her father doted on her, and while he spent time with the boys and their sports, he also spent plenty of time with Nancy doing tea parties and daddy-daughter dancing. Nancy always wanted to play sports along with her brothers, but her father told her those were "boy's games" and instead encouraged her to be their cheerleader. But her memories of the family trips to Virginia Beach each summer as well as an annual drive through the Shenandoah Mountains to see the fall leaves made up for it. Life was good.

Even though the family lived their lives in a very traditional style, the world was changing. Nancy would never forget that Friday afternoon in 1963 when she heard the news that President Kennedy had been shot while visiting Dallas, Texas. She and her family spent that weekend, just like everyone else in the country, watching the events on their black and white television set. The entire country was in shock. For Nancy, it was particularly impressionable, as it was the first serious act of violence she had ever experienced. She learned that bad things can happen in a perfect world, and she knew that this realization would always stick with her.

There were also many good memories from her childhood. There was the time she swooned with her girlfriends on the school bus one February morning in 1964 after seeing The Beatles on *The Ed Sullivan Show* the night before. She would also never forget the warm feeling she got when Joey McGregor gave her a stuffed bear at the Mechanicsville community picnic. And she loved the pride she felt when she showed Walt and Katherine her straight-A report cards. She marveled at how wonderful technology was when she first saw *Walt Disney's Wonderful World of Color* broadcast on a neighbor's new color television in 1964.

The world was a changing place during the 1960s. The nightly news broadcast showed scenes of civil rights demonstrations, the Cold War with Russia, and Vietnam. She watched the reports as Senator Robert F. Kennedy gave the sad news of Dr. Martin Luther King, Jr.'s assassination. She was shocked when only months later, Senator Kennedy was assassinated as well. She remembered the Summer of Love in 1967 and man's first landing on the moon in 1969. Only later in life would she realize the significance of her safe and secure family life and how different it was from the world outside of small-town Virginia.

Nancy tried out for cheerleader in her third year at Robert E. Lee Junior High School. She worked hard to prepare for her tryout. Her heart was pounding when her name was called to go out to the middle of the gym floor and perform the cheer she had practiced. She went through the motions mechanically. Processes and routines came easy to her. She finished flawlessly and sported a huge smile on her face. The review panel thanked her and told her that the list of those accepted onto the team would be posted that Friday.

Nancy rushed to the gymnasium as soon as the dismissal bell rang that Friday. Her eyes quickly scanned the list and stopped abruptly when she saw her name eight places down. Tears of joy welled in her eyes. She already knew two girls who had been on the squad the prior year, and she was excited to meet the others. She was suddenly aware of someone looking over her shoulder. She turned to see a very pretty blonde girl a couple of inches taller than herself. She recognized her, but they had never met. The girl saw her own name on the list and squealed with excitement.

"Sounds like you made it," Nancy said to her.

"Oh, yes!" the girl replied. "I just don't think I could go on living if I hadn't made the team." Looking down at Nancy, she said, "I'm sorry. I don't think we've met. My name is Dixie."

"Hi Dixie. I'm Nancy. I'm in ninth grade and I made the team as well!"

Dixie and Nancy became close friends through cheerleading. They were both friendly with the other girls on the team, but there was a special bond between the two of them. They started going everywhere together, especially when they knew there would be boys present. Even though they became the best of friends, Dixie was very different from Nancy. Where Nancy had been brought up in a traditionally conservative southern family, Dixie's family was much more liberal. Her father had campaigned hard for Hubert Humphrey, a democrat, in the conservative state of Virginia. His construction business was very successful, and he provided his children with just about anything they wanted. For Dixie's sixteenth birthday, he gave her a new Ford Mustang Shelby Cobra. Dixie referred to herself as a "flower child" and gravitated to all of the new fashions. She also had one of the best collections of rock 'n' roll albums of all their friends.

Even though Dixie had many material possessions, she still seemed to be missing something in her life. She often told Nancy that she was the only person that she felt comfortable opening up with. In a way, Nancy felt sorry for her friend, but she learned to more greatly appreciate her own home life. She recognized that Dixie's values were based on being a free spirit. She had not been taught to make good life decisions. Nancy vowed to try to be there for Dixie anytime she needed someone. The girls would spend long hours in Dixie's basement where she had made herself a "hippie pad" complete with hanging beads, black lights, and posters. It was there that Nancy started to see her friend slipping away.

One rainy Saturday afternoon during their junior year at Robert E. Lee, Dixie asked Nancy if she could keep a secret. Nancy told her that was a silly thing to ask and of course she could. Dixie opened the little bag that she wore around her neck. Nancy's eyes opened wide at the sight of the marijuana cigarette in Dixie's hand. Although she had never considered herself prudish, the sight of this illegal drug made her extremely nervous.

"What are you going to do with that?" Nancy asked nervously.

"What do you think, silly?" Dixie replied. "I got it for us."

Nancy was stunned. She loved her friend but knew that she couldn't compromise everything she had been taught to do something illegal. "I'm sorry, Dixie," she stammered, "but I can't do this. I need to go." Nancy gathered her things as Dixie sat alone and lit the joint. Things between them would never be the same after that day. Nancy remained casually friendly with Dixie, but she realized that their worlds were very far apart. During their senior year of high school, a band from California came through the Richmond area. The lead guitarist told Dixie, "California is the place you ought to be." She became enamored with the thought of living among the Haight-Ashbury hippie scene and left school to travel the country. That was the last time Nancy ever saw her friend.

Nancy graduated high school as a member of the National Honor Society in May of 1972. Her academic achievements got her accepted to Duke University. She enrolled there in the fall of 1972 with the intentions of becoming a teacher. She adapted to college life easily and continued with her academic success. Life was good and it got even better in the middle of her second semester when she met a guy named Jim. Jim Underhill was a good-looking Southern boy from Natchez, Mississippi. His family came from old money. He was older than Nancy and planned to graduate with a premed degree at the end of that semester. He had already been accepted into Duke Medical School. Nancy was in love.

Nancy and Jim were married in the summer of 1974 and began living the American Dream. They both came from solid homes and had been taught that a college education and a career could provide them with even more than their parents had achieved. They moved into a small apartment to save money and Nancy got a part-time job to help with expenses. As Jim moved further into med school, the bills started to pile up. Medical school was more expensive than either of them anticipated. In the middle of her junior year, Nancy made the decision to put her education on hold and get a full-time job to help manage their growing debt. She found a job in a retail clothing store. The time on her feet was exhausting, and the hours varied each week, but she knew her contribution to the new family's effort was worth the price[2]. Nancy eventually worked her way up to assistant manager of the store. She knew, however, that it was as far as she could go because the owner's son would always have the title of manager.

In March of 1978 Nancy told Jim that they were going to have a baby. In April of 1978, Jim told Nancy that he wanted a divorce. She had trusted him with her heart, but loyalty and honesty were not his strengths. He had fallen in love with one of the medical assistants at the hospital and was going to follow his heart. Nancy was devastated. She fell into a deep depression and worried how she would provide for

---

[2]   The baby boomer generation initially had a strong sense of family before self. Although many of this generation turned to the "hippie" movement and embraced the "tune in, turn on, and drop out (of society)," the majority held to traditional values. Many of those who were a part of the Cultural Revolution eventually realized that it would not provide long-term fulfillment. These people eventually became the "Yuppies" of the '80s and '90s.

herself and her new baby on her own. As she slowly worked through the situation and gathered her strength, she resolved to never again allow herself to sacrifice her own dreams in order to appease someone else. Nancy would become self-reliant, endeavoring to accomplish what she knew she could do. Her daughter, Jennifer, was born the day before Christmas.

In January of 1979 Nancy received word that her old friend Dixie had died of a heroin overdose in San Francisco. The sadness that she hadn't been able to save Dixie pained her. Nancy cried. She reflected on how our values influence our decisions and how our decisions impact our lives.

By the spring of 1979, Nancy realized that she would need to finish her college education if she was going to build a new life. She moved back to Richmond and applied to Virginia Commonwealth University's School of Business. Walt and Katherine stood behind her and helped out however they could. Katherine kept Jennifer while Nancy attended class, and Walt made sure that the bills didn't get out of control. Nancy loved her parents but hated that she had to rely on their help at this point in her life. This only strengthened her resolve to take total control of her life and her surroundings. She worked hard and graduated in the spring of 1981. She landed a position with Dominion Energy in Richmond as a business analyst.

Nancy worked hard and soon realized that she had an intense interest in project management. Like most people her age, she was a workaholic and lived to work. While working sixty hours a week and taking care of Jennifer, she finished her Project Management Professional certification in 1982. She felt confident that she would be able to move up to a project manager position at the first opportunity. It wasn't long before a position was posted on the company's job bulletin board. Nancy was elated and confident as she walked to the human resource office with her application and résumé in hand. She knew that she was as good as or better qualified than anyone at Dominion. Her feelings were reinforced as she passed through the first round of interviews and was selected for round two. But she was devastated when they told her that the position would be given to one of the men in the office.

It was becoming apparent to Nancy that in order to get ahead in a "man's world" she would need to continually increase her knowledge and experience. She began to work more hours and enrolled at Virginia Commonwealth University to pursue her MBA. The times were "a-changing," and Nancy began to see that the traditional values she grew up with would no longer help her in a changing world. Although she was loyal to the company, she began to question the traditional authority channels within the business. Nancy set her mind on providing a new world for Jennifer—a place where she would always be safe and have everything she needed and also have the opportunity to experience things without being limited because she was female. As Nancy had learned from her father, she was confident that hard work would pay off for her and her daughter.

What shaped the baby boomer generation:

- Civil rights movement
- Cold War with Russia
- The Space Race
- Vietnam
- Sexual revolution
- Growing violence/leader assassinations
- The belief in the American Dream—that if you work hard enough and long enough, you can achieve anything you want
- Woodstock and the explosion of rock 'n' roll
- Strong family life growing up
- Television
- Jet airliners/Interstate highway system completed/expanded travel
- Political scandals/lack of trust in traditional politicians/ Watergate/President Nixon resigns

Framework of the workplace as they entered the job market:

- Men generally went into trades or professional tracks
- Women were generally expected to be teachers, secretaries, nurses, or homemakers
- Glass ceiling for women
- Communication was done face-to-face or by telephone. Messages were delivered on message pads. Dictation and shorthand were common.
- "Climb the corporate ladder"
- Iron-fisted hierarchical leadership
- Technology was a productive tool instead of a use for connectivity
- Growing number of degreed professionals
- "Big business" was growing (OPEC, energy companies, insurance companies, pharmaceuticals)
- Business was conducted in offices; sales were done in retail stores or "on the road"
- Early innovation of impactful businesses (FedEx, Southwest Airlines, Microsoft, Apple)
- Divorce and single parents in the workplace were becoming common
- Belief that advancement was based on experience

Work ethic and values:

- Loyalty to career and employer
- Loyal to a team
- "Play by the rules"/Innovation not encouraged
- Workaholics (fifty-plus hours/week)
- Heavy focus on work as an anchor in life
- Fear of speaking up regarding sexual harassment
- Questioning and challenging authority

- Process-oriented
- Value ambition, collaboration, equality, and personal gratification
- Want a flexible plan for retirement
- Willing to take risks
- Value personal growth
- Relationship-focused at work
- Want respect from younger employees

SO . . . WHAT DOES ALL THIS MEAN?

The evolution of the traditionalist produced a society that emphasized education and productivity. The baby boomer generation was ushered in during a period of growth and prosperity. In Nancy's early years, there was a decreasing concern for meeting basic needs. The average family was able to find work that not only provided for daily sustenance but also offered opportunity for advancement. Nancy and her brothers were raised with expectations of achievement. Education was a priority so that children would exceed the circumstances of their parents. Nancy's solid family background helped her achieve success both academically and socially. Threats to safety and security were minimized as Nancy and her friends would play freely in neighborhoods without concern from their parents. Advances in technology led to separation of status in the workplace. (The emergence of "blue collar" and "white collar" classifications of work status are just one example of groups becoming affiliated by role.) The development of communication technology provided immediate visual experience of world events like the Cuban Missile Crisis and the Vietnam War. The period produced a substantial change in social values, including philosophies of child-rearing, creation of the social welfare system, women entering the workplace at all levels of service, divisions in loyalty to various causes, to mention only a few. Nancy's transition from a secure, supportive family to life as a single parent in a professional role, in part, illustrates the incredible social change experienced by the boomer.

Nancy's generational experience was impacted by significant changes in society. For example, the introduction of parenting theories that focused less on structured child compliance and more on individual expression, to some degree, altered the typical childhood experience. This lack of parental structure impacted children's abilities to accept limits and develop a capacity for self-control. We will explore this more deeply in another chapter, but children who experience clear limits set by caregivers are more likely to appreciate and accept boundaries. Nancy's parents were divided on parenting philosophy, and like many boomers, Nancy experienced childhood with aspects of both philosophies. However, her success navigating through the subsequent stages of development is likely attributable to her development of self-control and accepting limits. Nancy's friend Dixie who was raised as a "free spirit" appeared to lack a healthy attitude toward limits. Nancy's strong sense of identity during adolescence helped her pursue productive goals. Without a clear sense of identity, Dixie was more apt to take risks, affiliate with an unconventional (for that period) lifestyle, and experiment with substances that resulted in an untimely death. Many factors influence development; however, like most structures, the less firm the foundation, the greater the risk of collapse.

Baby boomers like Nancy had their basic needs met by their parents during childhood. Parents of this generation also became progressively more focused on meeting their children's relational needs. Nancy's parents grounded her in understanding the importance of personal care and well-being which gave her a strong sense of self. She was exposed to a strong work ethic which she modeled in her academic and career pursuits. Her love and belongingness needs led her to make sacrifices in her career path to support her husband's career. Then, when her world was shattered by divorce, Nancy focused on becoming the sole provider where she could gain independence and ensure that her daughter would have everything she needed. Her attempts to achieve advancement in the work environment were frustrated by stereotypic attitudes toward women, but she was motivated to do whatever was necessary to achieve in spite of stereotypical barriers.

CHAPTER 3

Bill, the Generation Xer

William Prescott Thomas III, or Billy, was born on April 19, 1970, to baby boomer parents William Prescott Thomas Jr. and Mary Kay Thomas. His family lived in Webster, New York, just outside of Rochester. Both of Billy's parents had full-time jobs. His dad, William Jr., was a production manager at Xerox and his mother, Mary Kay, was a human resource specialist at Kodak. They were not an affluent family, but they were able to give Billy the things he needed to grow up strong. Education was important to the family, and Billy studied hard and was successful in school. They supported him through Little League baseball and Pop Warner football leagues. He grew up with conservative values instilled by both his parents and reinforced by weekly attendance at the First Presbyterian Church of Webster.

Billy rushed home as soon as school let out one fall day in 1977. Two of his best friends were coming over to play. They were becoming known as latchkey kids—children who return after school to an empty home because their parent or parents are working. These children learned to follow rules regarding what they could and couldn't do as they spent time alone. All of Billy's friends' parents knew his mom and dad and felt safer having their children play together. Billy could hardly contain his excitement that fall day. The night before, his dad bought him the new Atari 2600 video game console, and he and his friends were going to play Combat until it was time for his friends to go home for dinner. He was the first of his friends to have an Atari, and everyone was jealous. He felt that this was the best thing to happen to him since he saw *Star Wars* in June of that year. He was without a doubt the most popular boy in his neighborhood, and he couldn't have been happier.

Like most of his friends, Billy paid attention to world events from a distance. It seemed that the things that were happening in the world were all very far away from his home in Webster. He watched with interest as Jimmy Carter and Ronald Reagan were elected president, Three Mile Island experienced a partial meltdown, and the Iran hostage crisis unfolded. It seemed to him that although these events were important, they really didn't change the way he lived. It was a good time to grow up, a time of relative peace in the world.

Billy loved his summers. His parents picked out a sleepaway camp for him to attend each year. Those were magical times for him. He was constantly surrounded by both new and old friends. They would stay up as late as they were allowed, then after the counselors were asleep, would all get together and tell stories. He felt a little sorry for some of the kids. Many came from homes that were not as comfortable as his. Some came from homes without much love. Some even told of needing to work as much as possible to help the family out with bills. This time away in the summer was these children's only vacation from a tough life. Other kids said that their parents sent them there so they could have some time alone. Billy became aware of so many things that he had never thought of; some of them reinforced values he was aware of from home; and some of them were totally eye-opening. All of them were helping him frame the way he would later look at life.

Billy loved sports, especially summer's baseball season, and he soon realized that he was developing an extremely competitive spirit. He had an intense desire to win in every situation. When his baseball team would lose, Billy would look to those he felt hadn't given their all and let them know how he felt. His coaches tried to dissuade him from speaking out, so he began to just keep his disappointment in them bottled up inside.

When Billy wasn't at camp during the summer, his parents arranged for him to spend his days at the local YMCA day care. This was much more low-key than the camp, and Billy spent long hours talking with new friends and the college-age kids who worked there. Again, these conversations with other kids helped him become aware of new things and new thoughts. He was surprised to learn that so many people he met had divorced parents. His own home, to him, was so normal even with both of his parents working outside the home. He felt sorry for his friends as they relayed stories of how their parent's relationships had deteriorated. He was sad when he thought about parents vying for power and control with each other over custody of their kids, something that he was glad he never had to go through. Billy spent a lot of time dwelling on these family situations. He was reminded how much his parents cared for him, his siblings, and each other. He vowed to always be grateful for the strong example of a harmonious life that they provided for him. He paid more attention to the way his dad balanced his work and family life and decided that he would make his father his role model for his own life as he got older. He learned that you could be strong, decisive, and firm in the business world while also being loving, kind, and compassionate in your home life.

By the time Billy got to middle school, he began referring to himself as Bill instead of Billy. He was maturing and felt that Bill would be a more identifiable moniker. His interests began shifting from family to friends, and he spent long hours at the mall, socializing, talking, and fooling around with friends. Every chance they got, they would convince someone's parents to drive them to the local mall. This was also where he first discovered girls.

Bill and his friends were at the mall one Saturday afternoon when his world changed. They were doing one of their favorite activities: hanging over the railing on the top level and making up stories about people they saw walking down below. They would howl with laughter when one of the boys would come up with a bizarre "life story" for a person they had never met. They had just finished laughing hysterically when Bill felt someone brush up against his left elbow. Looking over, he saw an attractive, big-haired girl who appeared to be about his own age.

"Hi," she said. "I'm Michelle. Who are you?"

Bill couldn't form words. "Uhhhhhhhhh," he said.

Michelle laughed and went on, "I come here just about every Saturday afternoon. I've seen you and your friends a few times. Do you want to get a Coke?"

Bill recovered amazingly well. He glanced over to his friends and they all gave him that oversized grin that said, "Go ahead!"

Bill and Michelle walked off to the food court. Bill bought them drinks and they sat down at a table. Soon they were chatting like they had known each other forever. Bill told Michelle about his school life, his sports achievements, and some of the places he had visited on their family trips. Michelle, who was two years older than Bill, told him about her family, her friends, and her love of music. Her parents were older baby boomers who had moved to New York from San Francisco, where Michelle had been born. She was named after Michelle Phillips of The Mamas and the Papas. Her parents were now divorced, and she lived with her mom. She hadn't seen her dad in a couple of years. He was traveling with some band and living on the road. Bill was fascinated by how different Michelle's lifestyle was from his own.

The two soon became boyfriend and girlfriend, but Bill never told his parents about Michelle as he didn't feel they would approve of the lifestyle in which she had been raised. They continued to meet every chance they got: Saturday afternoons at the mall, times when Bill told his parents he was going to visit with one of his friends, and any other

34

time he could make up an excuse to get out of the house. Michelle would often sneak cigarettes whenever she thought no one was looking. She always tried to get Bill to have one with her, but he would say no.

One Saturday, though, Michelle stole a bottle of wine from her mom's liquor cabinet and brought it to the mall with her, hidden in her oversized purse. When Bill met her there, she suggested that they go out to the service area and drink it. He was shocked and knew it was wrong, but he also had an irresistible desire to make Michelle think he was cool. He didn't want to do it, but he went anyway. After only two or three swallows, Bill began to feel light-headed. After two or three more drinks, he lost his ability to think clearly. Michelle laughed at him for being "such a kid."

The police officer was kind to Bill as he turned him over to his father. Bill's father was not nearly as accommodating. Bill explained the story to his dad with tears in his eyes. He felt terrible for disappointing his father so deeply. He gratefully accepted the punishment doled out to him, and he vowed to never again go against authority. This was a hard lesson and one he would carry with him throughout his entire life.

Bill graduated from high school in May of 1988. He enrolled at The State University of New York (SUNY) at Buffalo, and in August of that year, he moved the eighty-eight miles from home to college to study business analytics. Bill was a disciplined and avid learner, and college came easy to him. He loved using the Compaq SLT/286 computers loaded with innovative software programs like dBase, Lotus 1-2-3, and WordPerfect. He was diligent, responsible, and focused, and he had the commitment to excel.

One February evening in 1991, Bill returned to his dorm room after his shift in the cafeteria and turned on the news. He couldn't believe the scene playing out before his eyes. He watched mesmerized as the bombs fell, the missiles screamed, and the tracers lit the night sky over Baghdad. The media had been reporting for weeks that conditions were escalating within the Saddam Hussein regime and war might be on the horizon. Bill's thoughts slowly formed in his head as he watched the news coverage.

He began to feel a strong sense of nationalism and pride. *The US is finally giving that horrendous dictator what he deserves,* he thought. *We are so powerful. No one can stand up to justice. This should be a complete victory within a few hours and will make the world a better place.* "We have the might. We have the right." became his motto.

After college graduation, Bill accepted a position with Panelflex, a company in Muncie, Illinois, that manufactured a new concept of modular workspace units later called "cubicles." Business was booming and Bill quickly settled in to the workforce. Panelflex's work environment was very traditional, and Bill learned to assimilate into the corporate hierarchy. He knew that as he gained skills and experience, he'd have the opportunity for promotions as they presented themselves. He had the "do whatever it takes" attitude that corporations loved, and he fully understood that they were paying him to "get the job done."

Bill loved working at Panelflex. They were an innovative and creative company. By 1994 they were moving into creating and manufacturing a variety of ergonomic office furniture items. Bill was doing well and had earned two promotions by 1999. Panelflex made sure that all of their key people were equipped with the latest technology, so Bill was now accessing the World Wide Web using his new desktop computer with Windows, keeping track of his contacts on his Palm Pilot, and using a new 2G digital flip phone.

Bill began noticing that more and more women were coming to work at Panelflex. He assumed this was a result of so many people getting divorced. A few of his friends had gone through divorce, and he watched as their wives had won custody of their children and had to find ways to support them. He wondered if that was a trend in other businesses as well. Being a single guy, he appreciated having women around. As was common at this time, he knew that the guys at Panelflex would always be in leadership positions. He was also aware that the women were much better at planning the food when they had lunch meetings.

The increasing number of women in the workplace turned out to be a good thing for Bill. In early 2001, he met Jessica, a newly hired project manager. He was immediately struck by not only her beauty but also by the way she handled herself in the business. This time, he didn't stumble over his words and smoothly introduced himself. They hit it off and soon began dating. Then in June of 2003, they were married. Jessica was three years younger than Bill and had worked on establishing her career prior to settling down to start a family. Their son Jacob was born in May of 2007. By that time, Bill had progressed to the level of senior director at Panelflex, so Jessica was able to leave the workplace to stay home with their son. Once again, life was good.

In 2008, disaster struck the US economy. Corruption in the mortgage industry had created a bubble that eventually burst, and the financial fallout launched a great recession. The construction industry ground to a halt, home values plummeted, and many families lost their homes and retirement plans. Businesses began cutting back accordingly. Everyone who was earning a wage beyond their potential value was at risk of losing their job. Bill was no exception. In March of 2009, he was given his separation notice. All of the values he had come to trust in his life were suddenly questionable. He still believed in himself, his family, and the ability of the US economy to survive and thrive, but he knew it would be a long road. The "good life" that he had known up to this point no longer seemed so good.

What shaped Generation X:

- Dual wage earners
- Transfer of parental authority to a third party
- Latchkey kids
- MTV
- Sesame Street
- Hang out at the mall as a social center
- Increased divorce rate/single parents
- Energy crisis

- End of the Cold War/Berlin wall coming down
- Challenger disaster
- Watergate
- Iran hostage situation
- Reagan philosophy and assassination attempt
- Atari
- Three Mile Island
- Gulf War
- Computers (Commodore 64, 286/386, MS-DOS, floppy discs, bag phones, dial-up modems)

Framework of the workplace as they entered the job market:

- Women were expected to work outside the home/pay differential was normal
- Still male-dominated
- Change in family/life balance (having kids later)
- Workplace environment/introduction of cubicles
- Introduction of computers as working tools
- Introduction of early software (dBase, Lotus 1-2-3, WordPerfect, email mid-90s)
- Fax machines introduced
- Dot matrix printer gave way to laser printer
- Introduction of Palm Pilot (first portable data organizer)
- Expectation to do whatever necessary to accomplish goals
- Strong drive for job succession
- Newspaper as a job source (want ads)
- Telephone first level of communication, face-to-face second, later on e-mail
- Sunday blue laws changed; created a more competitive retail world
- Belief that advancement was based on merit

Work ethic and values:

- Do whatever it takes
- Outcome-oriented
- Self-first
- Entrepreneurial
- Confident and competent
- High job expectations
- Decline of organizational loyalty
- Strong work-life balance
- Self-reliance
- Early techno-literacy
- Focus on results
- Early brand loyalty
- Loyal to leaders
- Self-starters
- Independent
- Work to live
- Education as a path to success

SO . . . WHAT DOES ALL THIS MEAN?

Bill was raised by two parents who both worked outside the home to provide a stable lifestyle. Many Gen X children were introduced to substitute care providers either at an early age or through school-based latchkey programs to assist working parents. Education, particularly secondary education, was viewed as very important. Opportunities to achieve and advance were readily available to those with a higher education. Advances in technology led to the emergence of computer-aided education and virtual-experience entertainment. There was an emphasis on organized sports and social activities. Bill's intact family was different from some of his friends whose parents were divorced, whether amicable or not. Males and females competed at the same educational levels. Advancements in telecommunications increased access to information.

Considering the stages of child development, the introduction of substitute care providers for children at early ages certainly impacted the personalities of children. Substitute care providers ranged from relatives to large child care facilities. The degree of emotional commitment, child-rearing philosophy, and continuity of care impacted children's experience at each stage of development. Engaging children in organized competitive sports as early as four years of age also impacted children's social development and self-esteem. Parental conflict, divorce, and custody battles created a challenge to some children's emotional welfare. Emotional instability impacted identity development, social relationships, and decision-making.

With the creation of many government programs and social support systems, Gen Xers routinely had their basic needs provided for with little effort from the individual. Yet safety and security issues were a challenge for many Gen Xers, with family conflict, marital dissolution, and alternative family constellations impacting children's sense of security. Ready access to visual accounts of tragic current events had a profound impact on feelings of vulnerability. Relational needs were being met through a wider range of socially defined experiences. Relocation for employment opportunities often meant separation from family and friends to unfamiliar settings. Distance relationships, online dating, and social acceptance of casual sex blurred the line between intimacy and isolation. For those with a productive sense of identity, hard work produced opportunities for advancement and self-esteem as adults.

CHAPTER 4

Ashlee, the Millennial

Ashlee's would never forget the night her mother, Karen Williams, came into her room and woke her up to tell her that her dad would no longer be living with them. Ashlee, only four years old at the time, didn't understand what divorce was all about. Her heart was broken. She asked her mother why her daddy didn't want to live with them anymore. Karen couldn't answer. Her own life, shattered by the fact that Marty, her husband of ten years, was leaving her for another woman, was disintegrating moment by moment.

Karen worked hard to provide for Ashlee as a single mom. She knew that she would have to fill the gaps left by her ex-husband and meet Ashlee's every need. She bought Ashlee her first cell phone for her eighth birthday. Although it was a huge expense, Karen was terrified of not being able to get in touch with her whenever she needed to. They already had a Dell computer in their home, Karen using it for home management and Ashlee using it to play video games. Ashley loved technology and quickly mastered new games as they became available. Years later, as multiuser online gaming became popular, Ashlee made good use of the skills she had mastered to become an outstanding gamer.

Karen constantly looked for ways for her daughter to compete. Boulder, Colorado, was a progressive city. Broomfield, a suburb of Boulder, was where Karen and Ashlee lived. Their community was one of the first to adopt coed children's sports teams. When Ashlee was five years old, Karen enrolled her in both T-ball and soccer. She kept a calendar on the fridge to track all of her practices and games, and it seemed something was scheduled on nearly every day. Both her T-ball and soccer teams were required to have an equal number of boys and girls. Ashlee wasn't as physically gifted as others on her teams and didn't always want to work hard to get better at her position. Still, Karen supported Ashlee and constantly reminded her, "The score isn't what it's all about baby girl. There really aren't any winners or losers. Just being a member of the team is all that is important. You will get the same trophy as everyone else." Like many parents of millennials, Karen was mostly concerned with Ashlee's feelings and less about how the team performed. She wanted to protect Ashlee as much as possible from some of the hurtful things that she herself had experienced growing up.

At every game, Ashlee kept one eye on the stands looking for her dad. He continually promised that he would be there to cheer her on, but he never once actually made an appearance. Yet, she held on to the hope that he would come. Even though Ashlee spent most of her time with her mother, her dad was still her hero. Marty had remarried almost as soon as his divorce from Karen was final. His new wife, Rebecca, had a daughter from a previous marriage, and now Marty and Rebecca had a son together. Jonathan, Ashlee's half-brother was two years old. Ashlee found it difficult to compete for her dad's attention with a new child in the picture, but she never quit trying.

On the weekends at her dad's house, Ashlee stuck as close to Marty as possible. She loved the times when he would spend a few minutes focused on her, but his busy life made those times rare. His attention span seemed to always be short whenever she wanted to tell him about something she had done. She tried to be daddy's perfect little girl in the hope that she could earn his love, but all too many weekends she would leave her dad's house with a mixture of hurt and love in her heart. Karen was good at reading Ashlee's emotions and always made a point to be there and support her during these times. The ice cream they shared together on the ride home seemed to take away some of the sting. Ashlee learned to rely on Karen's guidance as both a mother and a mentor. And when it came to interacting with others, Ashlee was cautious, a trait she would carry with her throughout her life.

In the summer of 1998, when Ashlee was eight years old, Marty told her that he and Rebecca were planning a trip to Disneyworld and that he wanted her to come. She was thrilled beyond belief. She researched everything on Disneyworld and soon felt like a subject matter expert on the park. She was as excited about spending time with her dad as she was seeing Magic Kingdom. Then, two weeks before they were to leave, her father called her to say that she couldn't go. Marty and Karen had had numerous heated conversations about him taking Ashlee out of state. Despite Karen's love for Ashlee, she just couldn't come to terms with allowing Ashlee to go that far away with Marty and his family. Marty explained that it was just too hard for him to make it happen. "I'm sorry, kiddo," he said. "I hope you understand." Ashlee didn't understand. Her heart was broken, and her vision of her hero father was shattered. *Why wouldn't you stand up for me?* she thought. Ashlee would continue to love her father, but she would never again see him as her hero.

Ashlee remembers watching the live news feed from the school shooting in Columbine, Colorado, in April 1999. As a nine-year-old, she couldn't fully comprehend why kids would hurt other kids in this way. Then on September 11, 2001, just two and a half years later, she remembers when terrorism hit home. She was sitting in her fifth-grade classroom listening to her teacher talk about the industrial revolution. One minute she was in the room; then she wasn't. Everyone seemed to be talking to each other, but she wasn't sure what the buzz was about. Moments later, her teacher returned to the room and told the class to gather their things and get ready to be dismissed. As Ashlee was waiting at the front of the school for her mom to pick her up, she overheard one of the older kids saying that someone had hijacked a plane and flew it into the World Trade Center. It was only later on that day as she watched the news that the seriousness of this event hit home for her. Any and all resemblance of safety and security was gone. That day changed Ashlee forever. She now realized that anyone and any place could be a threat to her and her life. She began to watch more closely the things going on around her. She paid more attention to people she passed on the street, wondering if they might be someone intent on hurting others. Her sense of trust in people she didn't know extremely well was starting to erode.

Ashlee's school years were marked by numerous events that shaped her thinking. The space shuttle Columbia disaster in 2003 saddened everyone's hearts. The capture and subsequent execution of the Iraqi dictator Saddam Hussein reminded her of worldwide political unrest. The Hurricane Katrina disaster in New Orleans brought her attention to changing global patterns and the fragility of human efforts in the face of nature. The mortgage bubble and great recession of 2008 caused her to lose trust in business leaders who she saw as self-serving, greedy, and uncaring.

The fear and distrust Ashlee developed from what was happening in the world made her uncomfortable around most people, and she had trouble making friends. She much preferred to retreat to the safety of online relationships. She did, however, fall in with a small group of girls from her school. Ashlee approached these new friends with caution, having learned to distrust until trust was earned. The girls introduced themselves as Emily, Cloe, and Rachel. As time went on and the girls became closer, Ashlee learned that they were a lot like her in some ways and very different in others. Ashlee developed a special bond with Emily's family. Her parents were also divorced, and she talked to her friends about her mother's lack of attention. Cloe's family was close-knit; however, her parents had strict rules around things she could and couldn't do. Finally, Rachel's mother had passed away when Rachel was only five years old, and her dad never really got over that loss.

Rachel's father strongly believed in giving back to the community. He was a regular contributor to organizations like Habitat for Humanity and Charity: Water. He regularly took his family to pack food boxes for Meals on Wheels. The girls, especially Ashlee, would go along and help whenever possible. Ashlee loved the feeling of contributing to someone else's needs. She realized that she could help to provide a sense of meaning to a world that had thus far shown her very little of that. She quickly became a regular volunteer at any event she could. Karen loved the fact that her little girl was becoming so socially conscious. Ashlee loved the fact that she had found a new place to fit in.

Ashlee's friendship with Cloe, Rachel, and Emily continued to grow. In her senior year of high school, Ashlee's dad gave her a new Apple iPhone. She was already an avid Facebook user and this new device would allow her to be connected everywhere she went. She was amazed by the new technology available right in the palm of her hand. The other girls now had smartphones as well, and their connection grew deeper through new social media applications. The ease of communication via the internet also allowed her to "get connected" to a new boy. Michael was two years older than Ashlee. Ashlee commonly brought Michael along with her when she hung out with her friends, and the other girls did the same with the guys they met.

It was there that the betrayal of friendship surfaced. It began on a Saturday morning in December when she opened Facebook to look at her news feed. Stunned, she stared at a picture of Michael and her friend Emily together. Emily's caption—"Me and Michael . . . Should I change my status?"—brought tears to Ashlee's eyes. She was shocked and felt helpless. Not knowing what else to do, she called Cloe. Cloe answered the phone and casually told Ashlee that Emily believed Michael was too good for her, and she wanted him for herself. The other girls were all aware of what was happening, but Emily was their friend before they met Ashlee. Ashlee was stunned. Tears welled up in her eyes. Not only had she lost the only boy she had ever felt comfortable enough to open up to, but she had also lost one of her closest friends. What had she done to deserve this? Why would they treat her this way? Ashlee decided right then and there that she would never trust people that deeply again. She would retreat into the world of technology where she could be in control and protect herself.

Ashlee's mother had always told her, "Just go to college, baby. An education will make everything all right." So, her senior year, Ashlee enrolled in the College of Engineering and Applied Science at The University of Colorado in Colorado Springs. She planned to major in computer science. From the first semester on, she worked hard on her academic path and she loved the feeling of success. The team projects in which she participated received raving accolades. She also regularly found time to volunteer in the community and loved that her schedule allowed her opportunities to give back to those less fortunate than herself. Ashlee graduated with a bachelor's degree in the spring of 2012. She was well on her way to a successful career . . . with a huge pile of student loan debt as the price of her education.

Ashlee had targeted her employer of choice—a start-up tech support business run by a promising entrepreneur who had created a name for himself in the industry. She had read an article on him while researching potential employers and was quickly enamored with the way he had structured his business. She was sure that the openness and flexible environment he had created would be a place where she could thrive. After going through a grueling application and interview process, Ashlee received the news that they had chosen another candidate. When she asked for feedback, she was only told that they felt the other candidate was a better cultural fit for the company.

Her next choice of employment was a well-established IT help desk business that was starting a new division. Ashlee revisited her résumé to make sure her qualifications met the needs listed in the online job description and application. She was both excited and anxious as she hit the submit button. Within hours, she received an e-mail from the company. It read: "Thank you for applying. At this time, we are not considering other candidates. Please continue to follow our job board and apply again if you see a position of interest." Ashlee didn't understand how this could be. She was certain that she had used words that would be "hits" in their keyword recognition software.

Ashlee's next lead came from her previous student advisor at the University of Colorado. She had heard about a firm in Austin, Texas, that had just purchased a smaller firm and was looking to rapidly grow it into a global information technology and support business. Her advisor knew one of the key people charged with making this happen. He had called to ask if she was aware of any talent that could come onboard and become part of the new team. Her advisor immediately thought of Ashlee. She said that she would be a perfect fit for what they needed. The interview process went quickly, and Ashlee landed the job.

Ashlee's first day at Cooper & Sutton was Friday, August 18, 2012. She was glad that she had been able to do all of her pre-employment paperwork through the company's web portal and she had been able to do her onboarding with a large group of fellow new hires from her apartment via Skype. She still didn't feel comfortable around people she didn't know well, so this digital space felt safer to her. Cooper & Sutton had given her a powerful new MacBook Pro. She was impressed by the amount of internal security installed on it. Once she had all of her login credentials, she was able to work wirelessly from anywhere that had internet availability. She spent a big chunk of the day listening to someone share about the company culture, plans, vision, and mission, which far outweighed the boring review of the office requirements, handbook, non-competes, and required HR online training. When the day ended, she was excited to have the rest of the weekend to settle in and begin to explore Austin.

The following Monday, Ashlee felt pride as she badged herself into the front lobby. She had a sense of security as she approached the guard at the front desk. After she introduced herself, he called her new group leader to come down and escort her to their work area. Dan Michowski was a veteran of the tech boom era of the nineties. He had achieved the reputation of being someone in business who could always turn a profit. He had learned what practices and values drove profits as he climbed the corporate ladder. He had been hired by Cooper & Sutton to turn a profit quickly and position the company for an IPO. Ashlee didn't necessarily agree with some of the rules he had in place. She felt slightly uncomfortable on the elevator ride to the fifth floor. Dan's presence was a little intimidating, but she realized that he was probably considerably older than her dad. She knew that it would take some work for her to be able to relate to him. As they exited the elevator, Ashlee saw the work area for the first time. It was an open floor with cubicles, comfortable seating areas, and a large casual lounge area complete with recliners, TVs, a ping-pong table, and a foosball table. She particularly loved the café area with the variety of specialty coffees and teas.

Several people were sitting in the shared space, fully engaged in working on their own MacBooks. Dan introduced her to everyone, and then he showed her the cubicle that would be primarily hers but that she might have to share when she traveled. No one at Cooper & Sutton was required to work within a confined office space. Dan showed her where his own office was located and told her that, as a part of their "open door policy," she could schedule time to meet with him there if she had the need. He made it clear that he was much more comfortable within the confines of four walls and a door that he could close whenever he felt it was necessary. Ashlee thanked him and headed to her cubicle to arrange it the way she liked.

Dan's work unit was comprised of eight smaller groups of six people each. Each team was given an area of responsibility that would contribute to the unit's overall achievement goals. Ashlee's team was led by Dave Snyder. She figured Dave to be a somewhat older than her, probably in his mid to late thirties. She hoped that he would be a little less rigid than

Mr. Michowski seemed to be. Their assignment was to create a support network that could handle 24/7 help desk needs on a global scale. The team sat in the open space of the floor and talked through their ideas and where to begin. Then, they created a plan. Ashlee was still not comfortable with the face-to-face aspect of this environment, but she listened and made detailed notes. Her role would be to research and propose a communication platform that would best fit their needs. She went back to her cubicle, sat down, and contemplated where to begin. Her head was reeling. She realized it was 5:00. She pulled out her backpack, slid her computer into it, and headed home for the night.

Ashlee's first conflict at work came at the second group status meeting for their project. She had worked hard to do the necessary research for her piece of the project. She waited quietly for her turn to present. When that time came, Ashlee attached the HDMI cable to her computer and showed a slide with the bullet points of her progress. As this was her first presentation to the group, she felt uneasy. She wished that she could present her work on a social media platform instead of here in the room. By the third bullet point, she was aware that Dave was less than impressed with her work. She was aware that she was clearing her throat much more than usual, and she felt herself trembling slightly. Still, she stood her ground and finished her update. As she raised her head and glanced around the table, Dave said, "Thank you Ashlee. Let's get together at my desk following this meeting and we can dig into this a little deeper." Ashlee wasn't sure what she felt. She kept telling herself that she had failed, but she knew that she had done her best to contribute to the plan.

Dave was straight to the point. He felt that Ashlee's vision for the project was different from his own. Ashlee felt her anger starting to rise. *If that's what he wanted,* Ashley thought, *why wasn't he clear with his expectations? And why didn't he give me feedback along the way?* Dave said, "Look, Ashlee. We expect everyone, not only on this team, but throughout Cooper & Sutton to be able to carry their own weight right out of the gate. Do you get that?" Ashlee wanted to cry, but she held back her emotions. She made

49

a mental note to ask some of her other team members how they handled feedback like this. She thought about asking Dave why he didn't give her clearer work direction in their next one-on-one session, but she was afraid he would take that as her challenging his authority. Maybe she could ask him to teach her how he would have approached this so that she can use his approach as a model moving forward.

Ashlee went back to her desk and grabbed her phone. She opened Twitter and sent an inquiry to some friends asking for their advice. She started getting advice almost instantly, and it continued throughout the day. She started to feel a little better and began to reframe her thoughts about the situation. She was about to set down her phone when she saw Mr. Michowski staring at her. Not long afterwards, she received an email from Dave telling her that she needed to focus on her work and stop spending so much time on her phone. Ashlee made another mental note that maybe this was going to be a tougher place to work than she thought.

Ashlee realized that she would need to make some adjustments, so she set her mind to learning how she could assimilate into her new position—and quickly. She had always been a fast learner, and with a few changes in her approach, she soon began receiving praise for her work. The work group continued to make huge progress within the overall plan of Cooper & Sutton, and their workload was increased to meet the demand of the rapidly growing business. Ashlee found herself getting more and more assignments, often keeping her at the office long after 5:00. In order to meet her deadlines, without having to take away from personal time, she thought she might need some assistance. She tweeted others on the team asking for help, but they too were feeling the pressure of the demands.

At this point, it seemed there was enough work within the group to justify bringing on new people. She thought the concept through carefully and presented her ideas to Dave in their one-on-one meeting. She felt confident that she had covered all of the bases to make a strong business case for new hires. Dave listened quietly as Ashlee went through all of the benefits she had come up with. She felt confident that he would agree. When she finished, Dave calmly looked at her from across the desk and said, "Thank you for taking the time to think on this, Ashlee. You make some really good points. The simple truth of the matter, though, is we just don't have the budget to bring on any new people right now." Ashlee left the meeting thinking, *Cooper & Sutton doesn't really care about people. All they are interested in is making a profit.*

Ashlee found a way to get the work done. She was still pulling her weight with the team and they continued to have success. However, the increased time at work made it impossible for her to serve in the community as much as she would have liked. She hated hearing of volunteer opportunities and not having the time to be a part. She missed how good it felt to help others in need. Balancing work and her apartment was all she could keep up with; adding in community service time and her own personal learning time—things that made her life feel complete—just wasn't an option at that point. Her mother's insistence on education had conditioned Ashlee to believe continual learning was a measure of success. And while she *was* achieving professional success in her job, she was feeling that a part of her was missing. She began to wonder if the mountain of student loan debt was really worth it.

Two years into her position at Cooper & Sutton, Ashlee's commitment to her job began to weigh on her. She knew, like most women her age, that her career was her first priority. She wanted to get married and have a family someday, but she also didn't want to rush it. There would be plenty of time for that. Still, she missed having family close by—and especially being near her mom. They talked regularly, and every time Ashlee said goodbye, she felt a pang of sadness. As her frustration with work increased, so did her loneliness. Austin was a cool city, but she missed the mountains of Colorado almost as much as she missed her mom.

Daniel Hambrick, one of Ashlee's peers, had noticed that she was beginning to withdraw from interactions. He stopped by where she was working and said, "Hey, Ash, got time for some ice cream? There's something I would like to talk about."

"Sure, I guess I can get away for a bit. I have sort of hit a dead spot in this stuff I am working on anyway."

As they sat down at a table, Dan said, "OK, Ash, it feels like you are slipping further and further away from the team. What's going on?"

Ashlee took a bite of ice cream and paused. "Ok Dan, we are about the same age and I think you might understand. I am starting to feel like Cooper & Sutton isn't the right place for me. I don't think I'm ready for a lot of the things I am asked to do. And quite frankly, I don't think a lot of the older people like me."

"I get it, Ash. I felt a lot like that when I was new. I struggled with deadlines, systems, and having to do things on my own. Growing up, my mom and dad did most of the 'figuring things out' for me. There were times when I totally felt like I didn't know what I was doing. I mean, I could do the work; my schooling taught me that. It was the whole way the office works that threw me off. I finally realized that I had to learn some new ways of working with people. One of the big things that worked for me was getting one of the more senior people to kind of mentor me and teach me how the office works. Once I realized that I needed to look at things a little differently, I quit getting my feelings hurt so much."

Ashlee listened and processed what Dan was saying. "I don't know. I just don't feel like I fit in. But I guess trying anything is better than staying and feeling the way I do. Can you recommend someone for me to talk to?"

"Sure," Dan told her. "Let me ask a couple of people if they would be willing to help. I get that we missed out on a lot of people stuff growing up, but it's never too late to learn."

Dan never got the chance to help Ashlee. A week later, Ashlee's mom told her about a business in Boulder looking for someone with her qualifications and she offered to let Ashlee move back in with her until she could get settled. It didn't take long for Ashlee to make the decision. That Friday afternoon, she went into Dave's office and submitted her resignation. Dave was shocked when he read it. Ashlee had been doing so well, and he was prepared to give her all of that praise in her upcoming performance review. He told her that losing her would put a strain on the project and the others in the group, but Ashlee didn't really feel bad about that. She had learned Dave well enough to anticipate his defenses. She was correct. He attempted to sway her decision by complimenting her work and telling her that he would give her a raise if she would stay. Ashlee was prepared for everything he threw at her. Her defenses were in place. She had no trouble telling Dave, "If you had listened to me and hired the help we needed, I wouldn't have gotten to this place. I need to have a healthier work-life balance with more flexible hours or the opportunity to work from home. And honestly, I need a boss that spends more time helping me grow." Dave was clearly angry, both at her words and the fact that she was wanted to leave. He told her that he was disappointed in her, but he didn't really have a way to talk her into staying. Ashlee had already moved on. She was excited to move back home, be close to her mom, and start a new opportunity.

What shaped the millennial generation:

- Increased dependence on technology/digital media
- Smartphones (particularly iPhone)
- Typically grew up as children of divorced parents
- No Child Left Behind (2001)
- Terrorism at home
- September 11, 2001
- Social awareness
- Same-sex marriage
- Online gaming
- Ethnic diversity
- School violence (Columbine)
- Google
- Reality TV
- Great recession (2008), then economic expansion

- Police shootings/social movements that followed
- The Gulf War/Desert Storm
- Overscheduled children and overprotective parents
- Hurricane Katrina (2005)
- Extreme emphasis on college education, resulting in student loan debt

Framework of the workplace as they entered the job market:

- Tech integration/intranet/laptops
- Virtual/remote workplace
- Open (social) office space
- Video conferencing (Skype/Zoom/WebEx/Adobe Connect, etc.)
- Wireless LAN (work from anywhere)
- Ethnically/culturally diverse workplace
- Team work vs. individual work
- Emphasis on leadership training programs
- Conference calls
- Lounge/café/breakroom areas
- Recession-driven competitiveness/downsizing
- Social networking
- Communication is technology first, face-to-face second

Work ethic and values:

- Technology creates a flexible work environment
- Want to know "why" vs. taking work direction
- Sees learning as growing/obsessed with career development
- Likes informal work spaces
- Wants continual feedback and recognition
- Collaborative

- Achievement-oriented
- Social issues are more important than business profitability
- Highly educated
- Wants to work in a positive environment
- Lacks discipline/needs structure
- Work, life, community involvement, self-development balance
- Strong sense of entitlement
- Entrepreneurial
- Prefers a "flat organization" over hierarchical leadership
- Likes "meaningful" work

SO . . . WHAT DOES ALL THIS MEAN?

The millennial generation grew up during a time when many social norms of the past were starting to be challenged. The tight bonds of the nuclear family common in Walter and Nancy's generations transitioned into a broad definition of family structure, ranging from intact families to single-parent families to blended families to alternative families. The traditionalist's authoritarian style of parenting was now perceived as overbearing and was replaced by a more child-centered philosophy. Many parents subscribed to the philosophy that they were doing the right thing for their children by giving them whatever they wanted. Keeping kids happy was the prime objective. Substitute care providers became commonplace in child-rearing as working parents now wished to maintain a certain lifestyle. Expectations for children transitioned from helping to support the family in Walter's generation to outdoor play in Nancy's generation to electronic gaming in Bill's generation and finally to cell phone dependence in Ashlee's generation. Gender roles gradually became more fluid in education, sports, recreation, and employment. Competing to survive gave way to competing to succeed which gave way to competing for fun which led to everyone being celebrated in competition to avoid damaged self-esteems. Face-to-face communication (for the traditionalists) transitioned to telephone (for the baby boomers) to cell phone communication (for the Gen Xers) and, finally, to digital communication (for millennials).

Childhood development needs and the process of achieving them were very different in the millennial generation. Less-structured parenting during early childhood altered the foundational experience for developing self-control. At the risk of overgeneralizing, a case can be made that a lack of structure failed to give children a productive sense of self-control, contributing to impulse control problems and discipline issues in childhood; sexual promiscuity and delinquency during adolescence; a dramatic increase in failed intimate relationships during young adulthood; and spiraling credit card debt and a pessimistic attitude during adulthood.

For millennials, the absence of a struggle to meet basic needs resulted in entitlement, or the expectation that they deserved to get what they wanted. As technically-savvy individuals, millennials learn, communicate, accomplish, and achieve using devices and advanced methods for achieving creativity. They often meet their belongingness needs through identifying with causes. They prefer work situations where they are in control without having to accommodate the needs of others (i.e. the rise of the food truck industry). Changes in interest result in changes of satisfaction with the present, which in the workplace translates into frequent job change. Their focus on technology enables them to trust the internet rather than relying on talking to another individual. They can shop, purchase, and receive items without having to engage another person. They have elevated needs to be reassured of their value by others, yet they seek to avoid individual interaction when communicating.

PART 2

Creating Harmony with
Productivity in the Workplace

Everyone's a teacher; everyone's a learner.

CHAPTER 5

A Story of Generational Dysfunction

(Note: This story is intended to transparently demonstrate how silly generational dysfunction really is. It is not intended to belittle or mock any generation. All characters are fictitious, although the scenarios are adapted from real situations gathered through our extensive interview process as we prepared to write this book. Any resemblance to real people or events is purely coincidental.)

The Old Grande Advertising Agency had a long and storied reputation as a place where things got done and done on time. Located in Des Moines, Iowa, the company was started by old William "Willie" Wontwerk in the early 1960s. He had made a name for the business by managing an account that promoted a new product that was manufactured in the small town of Armada, Iowa. He was credited with coming up with the product's new name, the "Radiorange." Willie grew the business by being a staunch manager; always adhering to the things he had heard or learned made an advertising agency successful.

Willie's son, Wyatt, loved spending time with his father at the office from a young age. He not only developed a keen eye for great ads but a strong sense of the values that made a business successful. He learned his lessons well, knowing that he wanted to be an advertising man when he grew up. And when that time came, Wyatt easily stepped into the routines of the business, and eventually took over when Willie decided to retire. Wyatt was proud to be the master over "Old Grande Ad," as he referred to the business.

The firm continued to grow over the years and continually added new positions. Everyone was excited in 2009 when they hired a new sales executive to manage client relations. Mina Peasencues had a reputation of being someone who got things done. Like most Gen Xers, she was "result driven"; believing that you do whatever it takes. She had the reputation of being one of the most tenacious people in the advertising business. An expert every step of the way, she never stopped working hard to ensure that her clients were completely happy. She also had the reputation of being a great people person, understanding that relationships in the office were a key part of things working out well and acting as a skilled mediator whenever there was a conflict. Mina immediately brought value to the business.

The first client that she brought on was a car dealership. Jonda's Honda was new to Des Moines. Nick Jonda had recently relocated to Des Moines from Omaha where he had sold his hardware business to a large national chain. He had always loved cars, so buying a dealership seemed like a natural next step. Nick knew sales, but advertising in this new industry was beyond his skill set. He had full confidence that Old Grande Ad would be able to help his new business thrive.

The account was turned over to one of the bright young graphic artists on the Old Grande Ad's team. Lester Prophets, or Les, had come to work for them right out of art school. He was known for his creativity and for designing eye-catching ads. Mina felt confident that he could get Jonda's Honda launched in a big way. Les would be assisted by another young talented employee—Marcus Present. Marcus himself was also capable of being a lead on projects, but Mina felt that the new dealership needed a campaign done quickly, and she believed Les Prophets and Marcus Present would make a great team.

Things started to move fast at Old Grande Ad. Mina was fully committed in her approach to bringing in new clients. In fact, just two months later she and Wyatt brought in a completely different client. Marsha Brady's background was fairly common. She was a housewife from Ankeny, Iowa, and had been head of the PTO at her daughter's school. She was known to be a huge supporter of education and family values. Marsha had become disenchanted with the city councilman representing her area and had soundly beaten him in the election two years prior. Her popularity grew and soon she was encouraged to run for a seat in the state senate. She hired the Old Grande Advertising Agency to manage her visual campaign efforts. Mina knew that she would need to bring in an exceptional talent to help Marsha win. After a quick but thorough search, she discovered a fresh and capable young talent in the Davenport, Iowa, market that had previously worked as a community activist. She was not only a talented graphic artist, but she understood political campaigns. Ima Dunn joined the team at Old Grande Ad two weeks later.

Shortly after Ima came on board, Mina brought in yet another client, PuKi Pet Care Center. This was a non-profit animal shelter that specialized in finding new homes for abandoned and unwanted dogs and cats. Mina moved Marcus Present over to be the lead on this new client's campaign. Her plan was to have each of the three talented young designers play the lead role for each client and be supported by the other two. It looked like a great way to inject new ideas into the work and make sure that all deadlines could be reached.

The artists loved the scope of the work and were excited to have been given so much responsibility. They were, however, not as fond of Wyatt's strict adherence to what they felt were outdated rules. The first matter of business every Monday morning was a staff meeting in the big conference room. It started promptly at 8:00 a.m. and continued until Wyatt had covered every aspect of the state of the company's business. These meetings occasionally lasted up to three hours. On Ima's first Monday, she was not present when the meeting started. Wyatt asked Mina about Ima's absence. Mina told him that she wasn't aware of any details and had not heard from Ima that morning. Wyatt instructed Mina to send out a company memo reiterating that strict adherence to the established business hours was a requirement. When Marcus saw the email, he immediately picked up his phone and sent Les a text telling him that they needed to be sure to help Ima out. Wyatt Wontwerk's anger rose when he saw Marcus send a text during his meeting. He made a mental note of this as well but decided that he would talk to Mina personally about this behavior. Ima showed up to the meeting at 10:00. As soon as Ima walked into the room, Wyatt asked her why she was late. Ima said, "Oh, I had to take my cat to the vet. She hasn't been feeling well. And besides, I am not really too creative before 10:00 anyway." Mina lowered her head to avoid Wyatt's look. Wyatt Wontwerk took a deep breath and went on detailing the company's business report. The graphic artists went on thinking about their projects.

In Wyatt's office following the staff meeting, Mina received specific instructions from her boss. "Old Grande Ad works when we all follow the rules, Mina. I expect you to make it crystal clear to these kids that anything less than strict adherence will not be tolerated. I want you to have a company memo in each of their chairs tomorrow morning making sure that they understand how we operate here. Any questions?"

Mina went back to her desk to create the memo. She knew that this was taking away from valuable sales time, but she also knew that she was loyal to the business and needed to do whatever it took to make her boss happy.

Only Wyatt Wontwerk was still in the office at 5:30 that afternoon when Mina placed the memo in each person's chair. The memo read:

OLD GRANDE ADVERTISING AGENCY
EXECUTIVE MEMO

September 3, 2014
To: All Old Grande Advertising Agency staff
  (especially those of the millennial generation)
From: Wyatt Wontwerk and Mina Peasencues
Subject: Company rules reminder

The business leadership team feels compelled to reiterate the rules and requirements of working at Old Grande Ad in the following areas:

1. Regular work hours are from 8:00 a.m. until 5:00 p.m. All employees are expected to be present during those hours.
2. Cell phones are not to be used for personal reasons during those hours.
3. Attendance and full participation at all leadership-led meetings is required.
4. All assigned work must be completed before leaving work.

Please see me If you have any questions.

Always,
Mina Peasencues

The following morning, the young designers glanced at the paper in their chairs. Ima immediately turned hers over and began to make a grocery list. Les Prophets sent a text to Mina to ask if she was really serious about the last point. Only Mina never answered because she only used text messaging when it was necessary.

The Jonda's Honda ad campaign was off to a great start. Les had come up with commercials themed around motivators to buy a new car. Included were things like buying a "makeup gift" for your wife after you did something to upset her, buying a graduation gift for your daughter, wanting the status symbol of a new car after having credit problems, and needing to show off to friends with some conspicuous consumption. Marcus came up with the hook line that was a variation of the popular Beach Boys tune with the words slightly altered.

Help me, Jonda
Help, help me, Jonda
Help me, Jonda, yeah
Help to get me in a new car

Wyatt Wontwerk loved the fact that they had used a classic rock song as their theme. He told them that he was surprised they knew any songs from that era. He had no idea that all genres of music were available online or that his young team was familiar with all eras of music. In his mind, the only songs they listened to were ones to which he couldn't understand the words.

The Marsha Brady account was more interesting . . . and challenging. Wyatt was a longtime contributor to the conservative party that Marsha represented. He had known her and her family a very long time and promised her a campaign that would destroy her liberal opponent. In his first meeting with the team, Wyatt made it clear that they should "pull out all the stops" to position her as the people's champion. The team met with Marsha and her staff the next week. Marsha had a plan for how she wanted her ad campaign to go. She knew that smear campaigns had worked in the past, and she was adamant that one would work this time as well. It appeared to the team that Marsha's adrenalin levels elevated whenever she talked about discrediting her opponent.

Wyatt was as excited as a child at Christmas to be involved with her campaign. The younger graphic artists, however, didn't completely share his views. They saw her a lot like Wyatt—out of touch with things that they felt were really important. Marsha spent most of the time in that meeting talking about how she wanted to degrade her opponent as a liberal money waster, someone who wanted to give away government money to help people who, as she put it, "wanted to live on government handouts." Ima Dunn asked her how she would feel about public assistance if she were out of work and didn't have money to buy food. Wyatt glared at Ima, made a notation for Mina, and redirected the conversation back to the advertising. Later he called Mina into his office and said, "I will not have these kids disrespecting clients by asking offensive questions. At Old Grande Ad, we will always serve the client's needs, no matter what. That will never change. If they don't agree with the way we operate here, then they don't need to work here." Then he directed Mina to communicate that this direct display of questioning clients would not be tolerated. Mina placed another company memo on everyone's chair the following morning.

There was clearly a division between the management of Old Grande Ad and those turning out the campaigns. The graphic artists got together to look for a solution. They didn't want to support any negative ads in what they prepared. They had heard enough of those throughout their lives. Marcus Present thought that it would be a good idea to get some input from others. They decided to put it out on Twitter without com-promising any details of who was involved. Almost immediately, thoughts and ideas began to come back to them. One of the early suggestions was that they turn the issue into a movement. Once that was mentioned, hun-dreds of others chimed in supporting the idea. The team began to talk through how they could make that happen.

Since Ima was the leader of this team, she pulled the creative team together. They discussed the plan and decided that they would create a subtly positive campaign to which no one would be able to object. They would study the negative statements that Marsha wanted to use against her opponent and find a way to reframe each one into a positive about Marsha Brady. The team felt that if they focused on her positive family values, they could redirect almost anything negative about her. Instead of saying that her opponent wanted to expand government agencies, they communicated that Marsha was an outstanding budget-oriented person. She was an expert on "doing more with less." This was demonstrated by how well she took care of the finances for her own family and had helped several non-profits become increasingly successful. When Marsha wanted to say that her opponent was in favor of giving more money to public education, the team instead told how Marsha had organized no-cost support groups and an active tutor program at her children's schools. They focused on how she would support creating a similar network throughout all schools in the state.

They crafted a plan to provide her with a rallying cry and seed audiences at her speaking events with people who would use the cry to incite a rally. Once the plan gained momentum, they were confident that Wyatt would support it. After much deliberation, they decided that simple was best. Every time Marsha would make a positive point in her speeches, they would have the crowd chant, "Marsha! Marsha! Marsha!" The outburst of energy for positive statements would definitely overshadow the simple applause for negative comments about her opponent. When the idea was explained to Marsha, she was livid. "NO, NO, NO," she said. "I want this campaign to show the people that I am good and he is bad. I am the politician here and I know how politics works. Attacking each other is how it is done."

Following the meeting, the design team retreated to their work area to discuss their direction. They decided that they would follow their original plan. If they got into trouble, they would at least know that they had done something that was socially responsible. So they stuck to the plan and waited until the last minute to deliver their work. Wyatt and Mina had worried about it being done on time, but every time they approached the team for an update, they were assured that everything was on track. As it turned out, the campaign worked exactly as they had designed it to. Marsha defeated her opponent with a huge majority of voters saying that they were swayed by her rallying cry. Polls showed that her positive campaign was what the people wanted to hear. She gloated in her brilliant handling of public communication, positioning herself as "the people's champion." In one news interview, she even said that moving the campaign in a more positive direction was her idea. The young design team at Old Grande Ad gloated in their confidence and insight. Wyatt Wontwerk sat in his office wondering how they were able to change the face of the campaign right under his eyes. He didn't understand why things just couldn't stay the way they had always been.

When the next management memo showed up, the young design team decided that there was a distinct lack of communication at the firm. They collectively went to Mina Peasencues to share their displeasure. Mina listened to what they had to say and told them that she would take it up with Wyatt. Mina told Wyatt all about the conversation during their weekly one-on-one meeting the next week. Surprisingly, he was very interested and receptive to the idea. He assured Mina that he was on top of it and would have a resolution in place quickly. Mina was impressed with the way he took the feedback. It was not in his character to see other people's points of view.

The next Monday, the team walked into the breakroom and found a new "suggestion box" hanging dead center on the longest wall. It was a good thing that Wyatt Wontwerk was not there to see their reaction because most people's week began with a good laugh. Wyatt however was very excited to see what suggestions would be left in the box. He knew that all of the younger people would be gone at 5:00 p.m. sharp, so he waited until 5:15 before unlocking the box to read what notes were left inside. He was thrilled to find one suggestion card. It read "check your email." Wyatt wondered what this could mean. Then he returned to his office and logged into his e-mail. There he saw a message from Marcus Present. He had an unusual level of excitement as he worked through opening the e-mail. Once he got it open, he read the one-sentence message from Marcus: "Help us grow professionally." Wyatt Wontwerk was not sure what to make of it. He made a note to himself to have Mina address it the following day.

Wyatt briefed Mina on the situation first thing in the morning. Mina was beginning to feel like she was spending more time trying to buffer dysfunctional generational conflicts than doing her marketing and sales work. *Sooner or later,* she thought, *this is going to catch up with me.* But, being the loyal company person, she asked to talk to Marcus and the others. They explained to her that learning how to do new things made them feel like they were growing within the business. Mina listened intently and assured them that she would talk to Wyatt Wontwerk about the idea.

She was surprised a second time when Wyatt thought this too was a great idea. He said that he would personally lead the effort to add this new professional development program to the business. Being an advertising man himself, Wyatt would show the team that he knew how to facilitate learning opportunities within the office. The following morning, the breakroom had a large poster on the wall. It read:

COMING SOON!!!

OLD GRANDE AD'S CORPORATE LEARNING and DEVELOPMENT PROGRAM

Personally led by Wyatt Wontwerk
Watch for details and be prepared to grow your career!

Everyone was glad to see that senior management was actually taking an interest in helping them develop professionally. The team talked among themselves as to what they thought the program would look like. Marcus Present hoped that the business would be investing in an online, on-demand library of videos to help them each progress through learning opportunities that fit their individual career path needs. Les Prophets wanted to have everyone set up with mentors who could help them with things they couldn't learn through traditional education. Ima Dunn said that she would be happy with a program to give them constant and frequent feedback about how they were doing. She believed the best way to learn is to know what you are doing right and what you can do better. The speculation and excitement continued to grow.

The next Tuesday morning when they arrived at work, each of them found a hardbound copy of a book titled *Climbing the Corporate Ladder* by Jess Gettinbye on their desks. Wyatt asked Mina Peasencues to make sure everyone was in the conference room at 10:00 a.m. sharp with their books.

Wyatt had a huge smile on his face as he walked to the head of the table. He said, "You asked for it . . . and you got it. I am happy to help you all grow your careers. I read this book many years ago, and it really changed the way I looked at working in my father's business. Today, we are starting a book club to help *you* grow professionally just like I did. Each week, we will read one chapter and be ready to discuss it at 10:00 every Tuesday. This book will show you how to get ahead in the business world. I am confident that this will mean as much to you as it did to me when I was your age." The team sat dumbfounded with fake smiles on their faces. No one wanted Wyatt Wontwerk to see how they really felt about this program. Finally, Les asked Wyatt if there was a video to go along with the subject matter. "Oh no, no," Wyatt came back. "This is serious learning. It isn't a documentary." Les explained that they were used to learning through additional resources that helped clarify the subject matter. "OK," Wyatt replied. He had a contemplative but confused look on his face. "I get what you are saying. I will have Mina prepare a workbook to go along with the chapters. Mina, will you please have each week's study guide to me on the Thursday before each session? I want to have time to look up all of the answers before our book club discussions." Mina lowered her head to avoid letting Wyatt see her expression. *It always comes back to me*, she thought to herself. *Why do I put myself through this?*

The first discussion that following Tuesday didn't quite go as Wyatt had projected. The young artists seemed to not only have a firm grasp of the subject matter but they were discussing concepts and ideas that went far beyond the content. It seems that they had spent time together watching YouTube videos on the subject. Wyatt sat back in his chair and listened. "This wasn't how it was supposed to go," he thought to himself. "I am the leader. I should be asking them questions and hoping that they don't know the answers so I can show them what a great leader I am." He couldn't decide if he should be angry or hurt. The fact that his team mastered the content never occurred to him as a possibility. Eventually, he decided to end the conversation. "That's all the time we have for today. I hope that next week you all come with your study guides filled out so that we can stay on track."

On Wednesday afternoon, Marcus, Les, and Ima were sitting together discussing the merits of their smartphones. Ima was going on about how much she loved the new iPhone and Les praised his Google. As they talked, Marcus mentioned that he was planning a trip to the beach in a few weeks. Les said, "Hey, I'm going to be heading to San Diego for some beach time myself." Ima turned the idea of a little R & R at the beach over in her head. The more she thought about it, the more it appealed to her. Sitting on the beach, soaking in the warm breeze, and watching Netflix on her phone sounded like a great getaway. Leading the Marsha Brady ad campaign had exhausted her, so she decided to talk to Mina Peasencues about taking some vacation time.

Ima and Mina met on Tuesday morning. Mina was happy for the chance to congratulate Ima on her campaign success. They reveled in their victory, even though Mina still wasn't sure how they had pulled it off. After ten minutes of conversation, Ima said, "Mina, I have something I need to ask you."

"Sure," Mina replied. "My door is always open."

"Well," Ima began, "I would like to take some time off to go to the beach."

Mina contemplated the best way to handle this idea. She decided to be sympathetic but direct. "I can certainly understand how you feel, Ima. We all know that getting away to relax and recharge is really good for us, and we all need that from time to time. But you have only been here for five months. You are barely out of your initial onboarding period. And, besides that, you haven't yet accrued enough vacation time to take a beach trip."

"I don't understand. Didn't I do a great job on my assignment?" Mina was starting to feel her Generation X side come out. "Of course, you did. But that level of performance is what is expected of you. Performance and company policy regarding time off are two entirely different things."

Ima looked at Mina. Tears were beginning to roll down her cheeks. "But . . . that isn't fair," she stuttered. "All of the others get to go to the beach. I should get to go too."

Mina sat spellbound trying to calculate how to answer that statement. What she said was probably not the best response, but it came out anyway. "No one ever said that life was fair, Ima. I have, you have, Mr. Wontwerk . . . each of us have had things happen in our past that we didn't feel were fair. We just need to 'suck it up' and get over it. I am sorry, but that's the way it is. In a few more months you will have enough vacation time accrued and you can take time off, but not now. Is there anything else you would like to talk about?"

By this time, Ima was openly crying. "No," she choked out. "I am really upset. Is it OK if I take the rest of today off?"

Mina was sure her mouth fell open in shock. She felt like she too needed to take the rest of the day off. "No, Ima. We really need you here."

Ima went back to her desk and began to search the internet for business-related conferences that were in coastal cities. Before long, she found a graphic arts design conference and workshop in Corpus Christi, Texas. She carefully concocted her plan: turn the trip into a business event that would benefit her work at Old Grande Ad. This time, she wouldn't waste time talking to Mina Peasencues. She would go straight to Wyatt Wontwerk. She sent Wyatt an email asking if she could talk to him. Two days later, he replied setting an appointment on their calendars for

Thursday afternoon. Wyatt greeted her kindly as she entered his office. He was a little uncomfortable because he sometimes had a hard time talking to young kids. It seemed to him that they thought and talked a different business language from what he had been taught. He liked being able to rely on Mina to communicate with them. Ima presented her proposal to attend the conference, and Wyatt responded by asking Ima if she had spoken to Mina Peasencues about it. Ima said that she and Mina previously had a conversation around her traveling. Wyatt contemplated the idea for a moment, and then said no. Ima was shocked at the brief and direct answer. Attending the conference made so much sense to her. In her mind, she could get Old Grande Ad to pay for the expenses, she would learn some new things about her career, and she could still get in some beach time.

"Why?" Ima asked Wyatt,

"Because it isn't in the plan," Wyatt came back.

"But . . . why couldn't you just put it in the plan?" she asked.

Wyatt felt like he was talking to one of his grandchildren. He told her that he didn't feel this would be necessary for her to do her job. Ima had a hard time accepting that. It was just her nature to need to understand why things were important or not. The conversation ended in an impasse for Ima. She left Wyatt's office feeling even more dejected about her role at Old Grande Ad.

Ima Dunn began to give serious thought to whether Old Grande Ad was the best place for her to work and be able to balance her work and life. She felt like the company rules were tying her down. "There are lots of ad agencies," she told herself. "I'm sure that I can find a place where I can work and still be able to do the things I want." It was the beginning of the end, but she wasn't going to tell Mina Peasencues quite yet.

The team then turned their focus to Marcus's ad campaign, which just happened to create the most interesting dynamic in the office. PuKi Pet Care Center was a local orphanage for puppies and kittens. They took in abandoned or unwanted animals and worked diligently to find them permanent homes. One of the unique things about the organization was that they kept every animal as long as it took to find new homes and they never euthanized any of them. Many people in the community saw them as an important charitable organization. PuKi Pet Care Center worked primarily on donations and gifts from local businesses. The ad campaign would be a critical part of allowing them to not only continue their operation but expand into new buildings to house even more animals. All of the graphic designers, as well as many others in the office, were excited because they felt they had a civic duty to help the neglected and unwanted—even the furry kind. Even though Marcus owned the account, both Ima and Les spent time helping pull the creative side of the campaign together. A few weeks in, when everything appeared to be going well, Marcus asked Mina if they could talk. Mina set up a time when they could chat in her office.

Marcus went straight to the point. "Mina, you know that I have been here longer than any of my peers. I was wondering when I'm going to get a promotion."

"Well, Marcus," Mina replied, "that is certainly true, and the quality of your work is very good, but you have only been with us for ten months. Don't you think that we should wait at least a year before considering that?"

"Not really," Marcus shot back. "I have a friend who works at Mulligan's Auto Parts and he got a promotion to second shift leader within three months of starting there. I have been here a lot longer than that."

"I don't think that is really the same, Marcus. Retail sales and advertising are hardly the same fields."

"That shouldn't matter. People should get promotions regardless of how long they have been with the company. It's about the work they do."

"I don't think I agree with you on this one, Marcus," Mina replied. "And besides, there isn't even a Senior Graphic Artist position in our organizational chart."

"Well, couldn't you create one?"

"Not at this time. There isn't any additional money in the budget for it. I wouldn't even feel comfortable bringing this up with Wyatt. I am afraid we will need to let this go for now. If and when the time comes that we feel like one of you has progressed to a position of leadership, we can address it."

Marcus walked dejectedly back to his desk. Ima noticed the look on his face and asked what was going on.

"I just had a talk with Mina about the business. All leadership cares about is making money. I don't understand how they can put getting rich ahead of helping people. They just aren't in touch with what is going on in the world today."

"I get that," Ima agreed. "She was very cold to me when I told her that I needed some time off. I don't know about you, but I am starting to feel like no one in management cares about us at all."

"No kidding," Marcus said. "I guess I will just need to put up with it until something else comes along." Nothing more was said to Mina Peasencues or Wyatt Wontwerk, but the stage was set for change.

The month that followed was a busy one for the art team. All three designers were fully engaged in their respective projects, and all three continued to support each other as a team. One Wednesday, Les came in and excitedly told them that he had learned about a sidewalk art contest that Friday afternoon to benefit a local charity. All three artists quickly went to the charity's website to learn more. They discovered that there would be individual and team competitions. They decided to enter as a team and filled out the registration form. Then they spent most of that afternoon developing their design.

Mina called Les Prophet at 2:00. She was across town at the time but had just got a call from Nick Jonda. He was concerned that he hadn't seen a prototype for his latest commercial that was supposed to break that weekend. When she got Les's voice mail, she left a message to call her as soon as possible. She called again at 2:30 and left a similar message. When she hadn't received a reply by 3:00, she called his cell phone. Once again, there was no answer. She then sent him a text message. He immediately replied to the text asking her what she needed. She texted him back and asked him to call her. He could immediately hear the anxiousness in her voice when she answered. The first thing she asked was, "Why don't you answer your phone?" Les explained that texting was much more efficient. "When people talk on phones," he explained, "there is so much pleasantry that has to happen before you get to the reason you are communicating. And, many times the conversation goes way off topic and takes too long. Texting is right to the point. I can say what I need to say without all that conversation clutter."

Mina explained to him how concerned Nick Jonda was about not having seen his new ad. Les told her that it would be done on time and that she didn't need to be concerned. She asked him where he was, and he told her he was at the office. Then he mentioned the sidewalk chalk art contest. He told her that they had entered and would all three need to be out of the office that Friday afternoon. Mina was not happy. Although she tried to support the team in their community service work, meeting deadlines for the business had to come first. She reiterated that message to Les. "Don't worry," he told her. "We have a plan. We will all work together to get his new ad done on time. And besides, this contest is actually company business. We will be able to showcase our artistic talent to a lot of other people in Des Moines. Old Grande Ad will get tons of attention." Mina wasn't confident. She became even more anxious when Wyatt Wontwerk called and asked to see her in his as soon as she returned.

The walk down the hall to Wyatt's office seemed like it was a mile long. She knocked, entered, and sat down. Wyatt told her that he had just received a frantic call from Nick Jonda. Nick said that he hadn't been able to get in touch with anyone at Old Grande Ad all afternoon. He said that if his commercial was late, or not to his expectations, that he would be cancelling his contract with them. Mina told him that the team had a plan to make sure all was good with Jonda's Honda. She also told him about the team's plan to do the art contest that Friday afternoon. Wyatt

Wontwerk was livid. "That is not how we do things at Old Grande Ad!" he roared. "Mina, this is on you to get straightened out. I expect to see a detailed project update with the plan to get this done on time on my desk by close of business today. And those kids better be here on Friday afternoon." Mina tried to be calm, but her hands were shaking. She too was furious with her art team for neglecting the assignment. "I understand, Wyatt, but they seem to have their own agenda. They always come through but just not in the way we are accustomed to. What would you like me to do?"

"Just fire all of them!"

Mina left Wyatt's office feeling like she had just run a marathon. "I wonder if that's what I should do. This team is sometimes more trouble than they are worth," she thought to herself. She knew that action would not be the easiest resolution. "Having to replace a talented but not committed team is a lot of work. The amount of work it takes me to keep these kids in line is like raising children."

The art team competed in the sidewalk chalk art contest and finished in second place. Old Grande Advertising Agency was recognized on the evening news that covered the event. They also got the Jonda's Honda commercial out on time. Everyone soon forgot about the experience, except Mina Peasencues. Her stress level from working with her art team was taking a toll on her. She found herself frequently scanning job boards and wondering if she should post for new graphic artist positions. Maybe Wyatt Wontwerk was right.

The following week, Ima Dunn did not show up for work on Wednesday morning. At 10:00, Mina walked over to the graphic arts area and asked the others there if they had heard from her. They all said that they had not. Mina was a little concerned but went back to her task of setting up new marketing meetings with people she had met at her last networking meeting. When Ima was not present for work on Thursday and Friday, Mina was worried. Numerous attempts to contact her were met with no response. At noon on Friday, Mina went to Ima's personnel file and reached out to Ima's emergency contact person. Ima's mother answered the phone almost immediately. Mina expressed her concern for Ima as they had not heard from her in several days. Ima's mother was not concerned and told Mina that Ima was at the beach in Destin, Florida, a trip she had been planning for months. Mina was livid and asked Ima's mother to have Ima call her as soon as she was back in town. Her mother assured Mina that she would do that.

Ima called Mina at 6:00 that Sunday evening. She asked if there was something important that she should know about or if the conversation could wait until she was back in the office on Monday morning. Mina told her that they would need to have a serious discussion about Ima's continued employment at Old Grand Ad and that she needed to be in Mina's office at 9:00 the next morning.

Ima did not report to Mina's office that morning. In fact, she was not present in the office at all that day. Mina called and left a message that Ima's employment at Old Grande Ad would be terminated that day and that she would need to bring her company-owned laptop and phone to Mina's office first thing the following morning. Once again, Ima was not present, but Marcus came to Mina's office with Ima's laptop and phone. He said that Ima had brought it over to his place the previous evening to return to her. Mina began preparing the separation documents. At 11:30, Marcus knocked on Mina's door and asked if he could see Ima's computer. When Mina asked him why, he stated that Ima just said that she needed it. He told her that Ima was at her desk. Mina asked Marcus to send Ima to her office.

Fifteen minutes later, Ima knocked on Mina's door. She acted like nothing was out of character. "You wanted to see me?" she asked.

"Have a seat, Ima. Why do you think I would let you have your company computer back?"

"Well, I need it to work."

Mina was shocked. She replied, "Ima, you no longer work here. I have your separation documents right her to go over with you."

"What? I don't understand. Why am I getting fired?" Ima asked.

"Ima, you took unauthorized time from your work to go on vacation after we had a discussion about your lack of accrued vacation time. That not only violated company policy but it potentially jeopardized client relations."

"Oh, that," Ima replied. "That wasn't a vacation. I just needed a little mental health time. I was really stressed."

"I am sorry about that, Ima. But due to the situation, we will need to separate your employment. Please read over this and sign it at the bottom."

Ima started to cry. In a small way, Mina felt sorry for her. She knew that in Ima's mind she had done nothing inappropriate. Ima had never really understood how the culture of a baby-boomer-led business works.

Mina Peasencues was tired. Always acting as the pivot between her older boss and her younger talent team was exhausting. She wondered if other Gen Xers in similar roles felt the same way. It seemed to her that Wyatt Wontwerk always expected her to handle all of the difficult human resource problems. It also seemed to her that the millennial team members were continually doing things that irritated Wyatt. She hated being "stuck in the middle," but she continued to faithfully carry out everything that was asked of her. She resumed her search for graphic artist talent. And she never had to deal with firing any of the other young but talented art team. Within ninety days Marcus Present and Les Prophets were also working for other companies.

Dysfunction in the workplace generally begins with the letter C for communication. In the story you just read, ineffective communication is the central theme. The simple definition of effective communication is "message sent equals message received." Ineffective communication while frequent in occurrence is rarely the intention of the communicator. There are numerous factors that contribute to ineffective communication, including lack of skill in speaking or listening, incomplete information, drawing assumptions or conclusions prematurely, and generational differences. There have been incredible advancements in communication technology over the last fifty years. Boomers, like Wyatt Wontwerk, focused on communicating in business using face-to-face meetings, written correspondence, and landline telephone conversations. Mina Peasencues and other Gen Xers experienced the transition from telephone communication to mobile phone and then to cellular phone as a primary medium for communicating. While face-to-face meeting remained important in business, the use of facsimile and computer-based techniques, like e-mail, emerged as standards for immediate transmission of information. Millennials, like Lester, Marcus, and Ima, became almost completely dependent on handheld devices for accessing information through the internet and communicating by text messaging. Face-to-face communication expanded to include videoconferencing. New communication mediums such as Twitter became the new shorthand with emphasis on using images and symbols to communicate. Texting no longer required a keypad with the introduction of voice-activated messaging. In a brief fifty years, the science fiction of Gene Roddenberry's *Star Trek* television series that baby boomers grew up with has become the reality of everyday life for millennials.

The remarkable advancements in communication technology have outpaced the generational adjustment of the boomers and some Gen Xers, as illustrated in our story. The traditionalist influences on Wyatt helped him build a successful business through hard work and dedication. Wyatt was cautiously open to new ideas that would grow the advertising agency, but he expected his Generation X and millennial employees to fall in line with the business principles he had adopted for himself. For Wyatt, success in business resulted in esteem. Wyatt surprised Mina, Marcus, Lester, and Ima with his interest in embracing their desire for professional growth. Wyatt understood part of the message, but his assumption that the business principles from his generation would meet the wants of millennials missed the mark completely. The unresolved differences in business ideology between the three different generations led to progressively increasing frustrations for everyone.

Mina, our Generation X character, was raised with a mentality "do whatever it takes to keep the boss and the client happy." This attitude toward business was one of the prime catalysts for the significant advancements and innovations of the 1980s and 1990s. Desktop computers with towers and Cathode-ray tube monitors were transformed into devices the size of a postcard with exponentially greater capability. Mina's education and success in customer service catapulted her from producer to middle manager. Recognizing the value of both the boomer's work ethic and the millennial's creative potential placed Mina in the unenviable role of trying to bridge the ideological gap between Wyatt and the young designers. She found herself trying to balance the rigid expectations of Wyatt (because of her respect for linear authority) with the free-spirited individualistic mentality of Lester, Marcus, and Ima. The failure of the boomer and millennials to appreciate the values of each other's generational experiences created considerable stress for Mina. Mina recognized that what Wyatt, Les, Marcus, and Ima had in common was that they were all outcome-driven and experienced esteem from success. Mina's attempts to accomplish same-page thinking with individuals who were not motivated to understand each other's point of view resulted in considerable frustration and reduced esteem for her. Mina's gifts were in the area of producing rather than in building generational bridges. Even with a mentality of "suck it up and try again," Mina's hard work at trying to mold self-oriented employees into a company-first perspective was a recipe for diminished self-esteem and a sense of isolation.

Les, Marcus, and Ima, like many millennials, were more than willing to work hard to accomplish an objective; they just weren't interested in adapting to Wyatt's philosophy that they should work hard at following managerial expectations. Many millennials were raised without ever having to worry about their basic or safety needs being met (Maslow) and therefore developed a more casual work ethic. The concept of "earning" was blurred by the concept of "expectation" during the formative years of development. For example, is it necessary to work hard to learn the principles of basic mathematics when a calculator can produce the answer more quickly with less effort? Furthermore, in children's activities, if everyone is to receive the same degree of recognition (degree of esteem), what is the need for making a concerted effort?

In our story, Marcus confronts Mina about a promotion that he believed he deserved because his friend had received a promotion at his workplace. He appeared to have no appreciation for Mina's explanation that a promotion is earned rather than a rite of passage. A second example of millennial expectation was Ima's emotional meltdown when her request for beach time was turned down by Mina because she had not yet earned vacation time. Ima's determination to get what she believed she was entitled to led her to go directly to Wyatt with her plan to turn a training opportunity into a chance to go to the beach. When Wyatt told her that her request was not in the plan, Ima response was to have Wyatt change the plan, which illustrates her sense of entitlement and lack of appreciation for traditional business practices. Also consider the choice that Les made in ignoring Mina's calls regarding the Jonda account. In waiting to respond to Mina until she used a text, Les communicated that business needed to be conducted on his terms. His apparent lack of appreciation for easing the customer's concerns, because he was self-confident that he would meet the deadline, illustrates a disconnect in appreciating the needs of others while expecting others to appreciate the needs of himself. The gap between the millennial employees having their satisfaction needs met and Wyatt and Mina's understanding for how to work with them created a situation where all were stressed and the business suffered. Without a mechanism to bridge that gap, negative consequences were imminent.

To better understand the aspects of generational differences in the workplace, let's consider some phrases that typify our characters presented in the story.

Wyatt, the baby boomer:

- If it works, there is no need to change it.
- I expect my employees to follow the rules set for the workplace routinely.
- Hard work and determination produce success.
- Develop a plan and work the plan.
- Linear leadership is the standard for climbing the corporate ladder.
- If they are not going to comply, fire them and hire someone else.

Mina, the Generation Xer:

- Has a reputation for getting things done correctly and on time.
- Do whatever it takes.
- Work hard to keep the client and boss happy.
- Individual productivity invites promotion to middle management.
- Value the point of view of others.
- Recognize the value of using technological advancements.
- Suck it up and keep plugging away. It's my job to figure it out.

Lester, Marcus, and Ima, the millennials:

- Love a creative challenge.
- If you want to communicate with me, use a technology that I like.
- I respond to expectations on my terms.
- The old guard is out of touch with today's reality.
- I did well; I should get what I want.
- Employees should get regular promotions.

- As long as it gets done, why does anyone care how or when I do it?
- How is my work experience broadening my horizons and sphere of influence?
- If you are not happy, move on to something new.

Now let's consider what each of these perspectives can contribute to developing a successful business experience.

Wyatt, the baby boomer:

- Outcome focused.
- Understands the value of self-discipline and sacrifice.
- Organizational structure provides a foundation for employees to develop their individual contributions.
- Employee loyalty is a prized asset.
- Learn from what has worked and build from there.

Mina, the Generation Xer:

- Find value in what has been established and what is possible.
- Different perspectives enrich the effort when effectively blended.
- An effective producer does not necessarily succeed as a middle manager.
- Respect tradition; embrace change.
- Create belongingness to avoid isolation.

Lester, Marcus, and Ima, the millennials:

- Appreciation for the potential of technology.
- Constantly striving for recognition and validation.

- Energized when pursuing a cause.
- Esteem is an experience rather than an outcome.
- Passionate about their individual objectives.

The challenge, then, is for each generation to appreciate the perspective of the other generations and recognize the potential limitations of their own generational perspective. The chapters that follow will introduce philosophy, theory, and practical techniques to the aim of blending the assets of each generation.

CHAPTER 6

What Frames Our Thinking and Decision-making

Throughout this book, we have tried to demonstrate that generations are more than birth years. One of our goals has been to provide a framework for how generational perspectives influence the way people think, make decisions, and act in the workplace. We have described common factors and experiences that create a typical generational viewpoint. Within each generation there are many similarities of ideology and behavior. However, there are also vast developmental differences. Individual differences are the result of biological characteristics, education, child-rearing and developmental life experiences.

In the 1960s, Erik Erikson, a German-American developmental psychologist and psychoanalyst, developed a theory of human psychological development. In this theory, he identified eight stages of development that people pass through. These stages are highly influenced by familial and social values and events. Erickson's building block approach (we'll talk about this more later in the chapter) focuses on how abilities such as self-control, self-esteem, learning, motivation, innovation, and so on are important to success in the workplace. These may or may not have previously been developed based on life experiences. In the workplace, if an employee has the necessary foundational skills, those skills can be enhanced. If the employee lacks foundational skills, they can still be facilitated and developed by a strong workplace leader. It is critical that leaders understand their importance and why a person might be underdeveloped.

The story that follows illustrates how parental influences can shape the behaviors of children as they move into and through adulthood and into the workplace. These two families from different backgrounds and child-rearing practices will show how individuals become prepared to enter the workplace as well as what contributes to both their successes and struggles. Although this story takes place with Generation X parents and millennial children, the same factors have similar influence in every generation.

A STORY OF TWO NEIGHBORS

The Tran family relocated to Los Angeles early in 1971. Thien Tran had been a government official supporting Nguyen Van Thieu and the South Vietnamese government in Saigon. As it became apparent that the country could no longer be defended from the Communist forces from the north, Thien gathered his wife, Thuong, and their two small children, Lien who was five and Duc who was two, and fled the country. They arrived in the United States with nothing but the clothing they packed in their haste to leave. Initial struggles led to success for Thien, who had a degree in education. He knew that he would need a plan in order to raise his family back to the level of life to which they had grown accustomed.

Thien focused on rebuilding his life in his adopted country while maintaining the traditions of his native land. His focus and work ethic helped him find success, and within four years he was employed in an advanced administrative position at the University of Southern California. He didn't need to think twice when he was asked to interview for the superintendent of schools in the Westerville, Ohio, school system. Westerville was a small but exclusive suburb of Columbus. He accepted the position as soon as the offer was tendered. Life there would be drastically different from Southern California, but then again life in Southern California had been drastically different from home in Vietnam. The family moved to Ohio and began the assimilation into Midwestern life. With their father's insistence that education was the key to success, Lien and Duc thrived in their school system. Both children chose to take on new Americanized names. Lien was now known as Lydia, and Duc's friends called him Daniel. The conservative values that had helped them along their journey became the model for family success.

The years ahead brought the family continued security and by 1989 Daniel was enrolled at Ohio State University. His major field of study was business and economics. The life lessons he had learned from his parents helped him excel. He graduated with highest honors in 1990 and quickly accepted a position with Cardinal Health. He married and he and his new wife, Sharon, moved to the bedroom community of Powell where they bought a nice but conservative home on a cul-de-sac in the Shawnee Hills area. Baby Brandon was born in April of 1992. Jessica would follow two years later.

The Martin family lived across the street from the Tran family. They had been one of the original purchasers when the subdivision was started three years earlier. Jerry Martin was an insurance agent with Safe Auto Insurance Company. His wife, Evelyn, was employed as a human resource business consultant at Riverside Methodist Hospital. Jerry was the son of a steelworker from Cleveland. He had been raised in the tough blue-collar world on the shores of Lake Erie. Jerry's mother stayed home with the four children while his father went to work early and returned late. Even as a young child, Jerry vowed to escape from that life and create a home where his children could have all of the liberties that he desired while growing up. Jerry met Evelyn during his third year at Cleveland State University. He was a business major; she was studying psychology. They quickly became inseparable. Evelyn loved Jerry's enthusiasm and motivation. Jerry always said that he needed Evelyn to keep him grounded. Shortly after graduation, Jerry accepted the position with Safe Auto. He was a natural born salesman and easily became a top producer. Evelyn had no trouble securing the HR position at the hospital. It was there that she gave birth to their first child.

The Tran family came to become friends with the Martins when Jerry's Labrador retriever, Sam, ventured into Sharon's flower beds. Sam evidently believed that there was some kind of treasure hidden there by Sharon and spent over an hour trying to dig it up. Although Sharon was furious, Daniel captured Sam and led him by the collar back to the Martins' house. Jerry Martin could see that Daniel was quite upset. After much apologizing and offers for retribution, the two men retreated to Jerry's back deck to share a cold beer. Not long later, Sharon came by to see what was detaining her husband. Evelyn met her at the door and after apologizing yet again invited Sharon to the back deck. She opened a bottle of red wine. Although the two families were quite different, they found interest in each other's stories. Through the conversation, it was discovered that both Sharon and Evelyn were going to have new babies the following summer. Preparing to start their families set the stage for creating a bond of friendship. Sharon and Evelyn spent hours sharing and comparing pregnancy experiences. Jerry and Daniel spent hours preparing nurseries in their respective homes. Christopher was born to Jerry and Evelyn in June of 1992. Brandon, Daniel and Sharon's baby boy, came along just three weeks later.

As they were the first child for each family, Brandon and Christopher were treated like royalty. It seemed like the grandparents' cars were constantly parked on Bluebird Circle. The homes were soon overflowing with "everything necessary" to make the children happy and help them learn skills as quickly as possible. Thien and Thuong Tran brought Sharon gifts of books and other items that would stimulate little Brandon's senses and heighten his attention. Michael and Robin Martin filled the Martin house with toys that seemed to entertain the parents as much as little Christopher. Although both sets of parents held similar ideas regarding what their babies needed in order to make them both physically and mentally strong, they had vastly different ideas about how to accomplish that. Evelyn chose to put Christopher in a day care facility since both she and Jerry had busy work days. Sharon, for the most part stayed at home with Brandon. On the occasions that she had time away from the home, Thoung would gladly come over and fill in. Sharon and Daniel held to traditional Vietnamese guidelines about how to raise their son; Jerry and Evelyn took a much more liberal approach. The Trans sought out toys and activities that would develop mental agility; the Martins were more concerned about providing entertaining stimuli.

The neighbors bonded over cookouts, card games, Netflix, and wine. Before long, Sharon and Evelyn were close friends. They frequently met up late in the afternoon to reflect on their day. On one such late spring afternoon, Sharon brought Evelyn a cold glass of Chardonnay as they retreated to the lounge chairs near the firepit in their back yard.

"Thanks, Sharon," Evelyn said wearily. "I really need this today."

"What's up?"

"I don't think either Jerry or I got a wink of sleep last night."

"Why was that?"

"Chris threw another fit when we put him in his bed. I don't know how such a little body can put out that loud of a cry. He went on all the way up to when we went to bed. I finally went and got him and put him in bed with us. That's what he really wanted. I don't think we will ever break him of that. Do you guys have that problem with Brandon?"

Sharon started, "Well, we did a while back. We were at our wits end too. Daniel and I did some research on how to get him to sleep on his own and came up with a plan we both agreed on. We made sure Brandon was very comfortable and content before we put him to bed. When he was in his bed, he did cry loudly for a long time. It was so hard to not run to him, but we knew that our perseverance would pay off. That first night was horrible. I felt like crying too. But every night it got a little better, and it didn't take long before he was going to sleep in his own bed like a champ."

"I wish we could get to that point," Evelyn replied. "Sometimes I think Chris will be in our bed forever. Jerry and I just can't take the disturbance. It's easier to give in than to fight him. We both are so tired in the morning. We will figure it out eventually. Can I get a refill on my glass?"

"Sure," Sharon said as she got up to get the bottle from the cooler. "Maybe this will take the edge off."

"Thanks," Evelyn replied. "One more glass and then I need to get back to start dinner for Jerry."

Evelyn and Jerry eventually got the bedtime routine figured out. But that was only one in a series of challenges they had with Christopher. It wasn't long before it was time for potty training. Once again, the two families had different points of view. Sharon and Daniel took a very systematic approach to helping Brandon master his bladder. They intentionally increased his time without a diaper, and they encouraged and praised him when he was successful. When the time came that he no longer relied on a diaper, they celebrated with him and had him personally throw the no longer needed items in the trash. Evelyn and Jerry on the other hand found it easier to let Chris make his own decisions about wearing a diaper. They figured that he would just be done with them when he was ready. To Evelyn, it was easier to keep him in a diaper than to wash wet clothes and sheets frequently. Chris learned early that he could get what he wanted from his parents.

For Chris's fifth birthday, Jerry and Evelyn bought him a Nintendo 64 gaming system. They took him to GameStop and let him pick out three games. They were excited that they had a new "in home babysitter." On the first day, they got to watch an entire movie by themselves while Chris learned his new games. Jerry told Evelyn, "This is the best thing ever for parents." The next day, Brandon returned from playing at Chris's house filled with excitement. He couldn't wait to tell his mom about the amazing new games that he played at Chris's house. He immediately began petitioning his parents for one of his own. Sharon and Daniel discussed it after Brandon was in bed that evening. "So, what do you think, Sharon? Should we get a game system for Brandon? It seems that all of the kids have one these days."

"I am not so sure that it is in his best interest," Sharon replied. "Let's do some research and see what the advantages and disadvantages might be. I like the idea as long as it doesn't become a replacement for reading or experiencing things firsthand." Eventually they decided that Brandon could benefit from having a system of his own. They learned that it could help to develop his hand-eye coordination and improve his cognitive decision-making speed. They did however also learn that the games played didn't have any consequences; if you "died," you just started over. They knew that this could lead to a lack of accountability, so they decided to limit Brandon to one hour per day of play. At first, he was upset with this short period of fun, but he eventually understood that it was all for his own good. Chris, on the other hand, was not given limitations, and later in life he suffered the result of not learning the valuable lesson of accountability.

The boys were natural best friends as they grew up. Their dads took them fishing together, they got rid of their training wheels at the same time and they sat together on the bus to and from school. Brandon was a natural when it came to learning. The disciplines that Daniel and Sharon had raised him with helped him to focus on his learning. He actually embraced his homework instead of wanting to rush through it and move on to more fun activities. Chris, on the other hand, struggled with making good grades. To him, learning was something that was required instead of a life benefit. He loved gaming more than his studies. Evelyn was more than occasionally reminded by Chris's teachers that he was not paying attention in class and that his homework was incomplete.

When the boys were in the sixth grade, they were introduced to summer league baseball. They both excitedly told their parents that they wanted to be a part of the Action Hardware team on which several of their other friends would be playing. All of the parents agreed that it would be a great experience for the boys. Many pictures were taken in the front yards the day they got their new uniforms. Chris was an out-fielder; Brandon was a pitcher. Evening and Saturday practices were initially filled with enthusiasm. Both boys returned home worn out. After the first week, Chris began to lose his exuberance for the game. He said that he didn't like having to run laps around the field because it was too much work. Jerry told him that he would not be allowed to quit since he had made a commitment to the team. "Just hang in there," he told Chris. "At the end of the season, you will get the same trophy as everyone else." Brandon quickly embraced the challenge of being a game winning pitcher. He understood that he could improve his ability drastically if he worked hard in his own back yard to master his pitches. Daniel was glad to spend hours with him, catching his throws and providing solid coaching. Brandon's work paid off. At the banquet at the end of the season, he was voted "most valuable player" for the team. He received an additional larger trophy to the one all the players got for just being a member of the team. Chris never played organized sports again. Brandon would eventually be offered athletic scholarships to five schools.

Everyone, including the two families, remembered where they were on that Tuesday morning. The reports started out as routine news of a plane crash. What was happening was quickly realized as a terrorist attack. Millions of people watched live as the second hijacked plane flew through World Trade Two. People cried. Some reacted with panic. Others sat silently as the devastation of what was happening began to sink in. Sharon called Evelyn at work and told her to check the news. Sharon had just gotten a call from the boys' school that they were on lockdown as no one yet knew the entire situation. They would be dismissing the entire school as soon as authorities felt they could safely control the situation. Evelyn was panic-stricken. She told Sharon that she was heading right home to get Chris from school. She soon learned that authorities were desperately trying to do damage control form all the people reacting much like Evelyn. Evelyn soon found herself in a traffic gridlock. Adrenaline was still coursing through her veins as she called Sharon and asked if she could pick up Chris when she was getting Brandon. Sharon picked the two friends up one hour later. Both boys had very intense questions about what was happening. Sharon struggled to provide answers that would help them understand without heightening their sense of fear. She explained that they would know more as the day went on.

Back at home that evening, as all of the day's events came to light, each family found solace in their own homes. At the Martin house, they all sat in front of their television while they ate their dinner. Jerry's explanation to Chris was that "those people over there are just bad guys. Muslims everywhere just wanted to hurt Americans because we have more than they do." Jerry told him that he hoped that we would "go in there and nuke them back to the Stone Age." Chris believed that everything was under control and went off to play Grand Theft Auto III. At the Tran home, the family also sat in front of their television as they watched the non-stop news coverage. Thien and Thoung had come over to be with their family. As Brandon's questions arose, all of the older people tried to help him put everything in perspective. Thien helped him the most by telling him about the political differences he had experienced in his homeland. He explained how movements with as much civil support often gain momentum whether they are good or bad. He helped Brandon understand that the people who committed these heinous acts were acting from their religious fervor. Although their beliefs were far different from the Tran families, they shared the same beliefs that what they were doing was an inspired act of patriotism. Brandon had a hard time grasping the idea, but eventually learned that sometimes bad people do things that don't necessarily represent the overall point of view of the people they represent. Brandon would see more of this throughout his life. As he later watched reports of movements like "Occupy," "Black

Lives Matter," Me Too," same-sex marriages, and even the Tea Party, he understood the passion demonstrated by the participants. He knew that he didn't necessarily need to agree with their perspective to realize why they were zealous about their mission.

When the boys were in their sophomore year of high school, the Martin family has a small crisis. Evelyn got a progress report from Chris's history teacher saying that Chris was failing the class. It seems that he hadn't turned in most of his homework assignments and that had dropped his grade below passing. Both Jerry and Evelyn were furious—not at Chris, but at the teacher and the school for allowing this to happen. Jerry took off work the next day to go to Chris's school and straighten things out. He was obviously enraged as he walked into the principal's office for the conference with the teacher. Jerry refused to accept that due to the failing grade Chris would need to repeat the class in summer school. He insisted that Chris be given special consideration and another chance. Against their best judgement, the administrators eventually conceded that Chris could get full credit if he just went back and completed the assignments before the end of the semester. Chris still was not interested in doing the work, but Jerry's anger that night made him fearful to not complete it. Sharon was appalled the following day when Evelyn bragged about how masterfully Jerry had handled the situation.

"Why would you do that," she asked Evelyn. "Don't you think that not taking accountability sets a bad example for Chris? I mean, what lesson is he going to learn from this?"

"The lesson he will learn," Evelyn told her, "is that you always have to do your work. Even if you don't want to, you still have to do it."

"But," Sharon came back, "don't you think he could learn more about real life by failing?"

"What?" Evelyn asked. "Why would we want him to fail?"

"Life isn't easy, Ev. You know that. We all experience failures at some point in our lives. I just think that letting him see what it looks like to fail—with something that can be easily corrected by a little inconvenience to his summer schedule—would be a great lesson for anyone. This way he can learn the lesson in a safe environment. It might help him learn how avoid this kind of mistake later on in life when it is more critical." "You know Jerry," Evelyn said. "He totally can't accept that anything could be Chris's fault. I kind of feel the same way. Besides, I couldn't imagine what next summer would be like having to listen to Chris whine everyday about having to go to summer school. He would be impossible to live with."

Sharon walked back across the street wondering how two families that had been such close friends could have such differing values and opinions on how to raise their children. *I guess it's like Thien said*, she thought. *People have their own ideas about life and are passionate about what works for them. I just hope that it works for Chris as he gets into the real world.*

When the boys graduated from high school in May of 2011, Brandon was proud to have achieved the salutatorian rank. He had applied himself in every class, taking enough advanced placement classes to earn credit for nearly a full year of college. Still, he was disappointed in himself for not achieving valedictorian. He had learned to do whatever was necessary to achieve your goals and make your family (and later on, your employer) proud of your work. He had scholarship offers from a multitude of highly recognized schools. Chris graduated in the middle of the class. He was still contemplating where he would go next in life. He thought that he would probably enroll at the local community college while he figured it out. He was still extremely passionate about gaming and was looking for a way to make a career out of the technological side of it.

Eventually Brandon would graduate college with honors in aerospace science. He would go on to work for NASA and become the leader of a team that would work with SpaceX to develop recoverable rocket engines. Brandon's parents and grandparents were overwhelmingly proud of him for his accomplishments. They continued to support him as he married his sweetheart, Sara. Together they would bring three wonderful children into the world. The whole family got together at every opportunity to continue the bonds of love, trust, and independence that they had instilled in Brandon throughout his life.

Chris attended community college for two years and then decided that he wanted to become a recording engineer. Jerry and Evelyn paid for him to attend SAE Institute in Nashville to learn how to do that. He found a job with a small recording studio on Nashville's Music Row. There he met an aspiring female country wannabe artist. They were married in 2015 and divorced eighteen months later. Jerry and Evelyn also separated, and they were divorced in 2018. They both continued to devote their lives to giving Chris anything possible.

Brandon and Chris exchanged Christmas cards and called each other on their respective birthdays. Conversations, however, were brief. Neither of them had enough commonality in their lives to carry on a solid conversation. They eventually drifted apart.

As we attempt to wrap our minds around generational differences and their impact on the workplace, it might be useful to consider a theoretical frame of reference. The characteristics associated with each generation vary along a continuing path based on the biological makeup of the individual and their environmental experiences. Physical development is a gradual process that begins with complete dependence on others and transitions to self-reliance. Likewise, personality develops gradually over time and is substantially influenced by environmental experiences. Generational categories (traditionalists, boomers, Gen Xers, and millennials) focus on common personality characteristics of individuals living during certain time periods. Some individuals within a generation will display many similarities, while others may exhibit very few of the characteristics generally associated with that generation. The evolution of generational differences is a gradual process where the personalities of those born at the beginning of a generation may be quite different from those born at the end of a generation. The story that began this chapter highlights how the developmental experiences of Brandon and Chris shaped individual differences of two boys raised in the same generation—even living on the same street. The process which produces differences in personality may be easier to understand by considering some theoretical aspects of human development.

THE EIGHT STAGES OF MAN

As was previously mentioned, Erik Erikson was a leading figure in psychoanalysis and the understanding of human development. In his book *Childhood and Society*, he introduced his concept of the eight stages of man also referred to as the "epigenetic principle." The stages of life identified a developmental progression of personality characteristics based on maturation and experience. He proposed a building-block approach to development where each stage of personality formation was directly dependent on the characterological development of the previous stages.

His eight-stage progression and the period of formation are:

Stage 1	Infancy	Basic Trust vs. Mistrust
Stage 2	Toddler Years	Autonomy vs. Shame and Doubt
Stage 3	Early Childhood	Initiative vs. Guilt
Stage 4	Later Childhood	Industry vs. Inferiority
Stage 5	Adolescence	Identity vs. Role Confusion
Stage 6	Young Adult	Intimacy vs. Isolation
Stage 7	Adulthood	Generativity vs. Stagnation
Stage 8	Later Adulthood	Ego Integrity vs. Despair

Note that each stage consists of opposing values ranging from productive development to unproductive development. Let's look, now, at the development of generational characteristics and differences and how they played out in Brandon's and Chris's personalities, social adjustment, and productivity. Then we'll talk briefly about how that applies to the workplace.

Stage 1: Basic Trust vs. Mistrust

Brandon and Chris were both born into caring families that provided them with a sense of safety and security. The critical elements of this stage of development focus on meeting basic needs of nourishment, physical care, sleep, and nurturing. When a child experiences their basic needs being routinely met, they develop a sense of security and comfort. Infants who are neglected or mistreated experience physical pain which inhibits the development of a sense of security and trust in their daily experience. The more severe the disruption in having needs met, the greater the impact on the development of the stages that follow. It is this stage progression that contributes to personality and character formation.

The stages of development that we see in Chris and Brandon correspond to stages of development in the workplace. Not all employees, regardless of their generational identification, have had the opportunities to develop their professional skills in all of the stages. Leaders with a strong understanding of employee development can help guide employees through the development stages and increase their generational interpersonal skills. Individuals who enter the workplace for the first time experience everything as new. There is a sense of both excitement and anticipation. First-time employees are dependent on established employees for orientation to expectations and acclamation to routine.

So, how does this apply to the workplace? Employees who are effectively oriented and nurtured through the initial phases of employment become comfortable with their new surroundings and are ready to explore their potentials. Employees who are provided little or no orientation or guidance, or who are misled by other employees, often feel overwhelmed. They make mistakes, and are subject to negative feedback.

Stage 2: Autonomy vs. Shame and Doubt

Brandon and Chris had different experiences during this stage of development. Both children presented a challenge to their parents regarding bedtime and toilet training. Brandon's parents used structure and consistency to help him learn to accept limits and adjust. Chris's parents were unstructured, overindulgent, and inconsistent which resulted in his testing their authority and receiving negative attention.

The toddler years feature a child's ability to physically explore their environment. An important personality characteristic that develops during this stage is a healthy respect for boundaries. As children explore, they begin to learn about limits and self-control. Children who have a basic trust in their caregiver and frequently hear the word "no" (to protect them from harm or danger) become increasingly confident in exploring their environment. This is a significant period in developing self-control and acceptance of limits. Children who experience productive interventions from caregivers become progressively more compliant with accepting limits and develop a healthy attitude toward themselves and exploring the world around them. Children who are overindulged learn to test limits. Children who are harshly chastised or mistreated for their natural tendency to explore develop a sense of fear and inadequacy. Children who struggled with developing trust in stage one and receive negative attention for natural tendencies to explore and test limits are likely to become resistant to authority or socially withdrawn.

In the workplace, employees who feel secure and comfortable begin to ask questions, try new things, and seek to be productive. When encouraged, these employees begin to look for opportunities to learn and grow in their role. Employees who have struggled in adjusting to the workplace are likely to approach new situations with caution and reluctance seeking to avoid criticism for not meeting expectations.

Stage 3: Initiative vs. Guilt

Both Brandon's and Chris's parents took different approaches to their children's interest in electronic gaming. Brandon's parents made a concerted effort to determine what would be in his best interest. They responded to his interest in the games and chose to have him learn to accept limits in the time he invested in the games. Chris's parents chose the electronic babysitting approach to get some free time away from him without be bothered. Chris learned that he could get what he wanted by manipulation, which, while effective, does not produce a positive self-esteem.

The early childhood years are a period of discovery. The maturing of intellectual processes leads to physical development, acquisition of language skills, and learning. Children who have developed basic trust and autonomy are extremely curious. Few intellectual and/or emotional filters are active during the early part of this stage so children are bold in verbal and physical exploration. Children who are encouraged to learn from successes and mistakes develop confidence and self-esteem. Children who are ignored, chastised, ridiculed, or rejected for their interests experience guilt and diminished self-esteem. Their curiosity becomes stifled and they begin to withdraw from taking risks or they may become rebellious which results in negative attention.

Employees who experience the workplace as opportunity begin to settle into their role, contribute ideas, and seek to demonstrate their worth and value. Employees who experience the workplace as a threat to their self-worth are likely to do only what they are told in order to avoid potential failure. They often feel constrained by the environment and their coworkers.

Stage 4: Industry vs. Inferiority

One aspect of the impact of this stage is found in how the boys responded to organized sports. Both were excited for the opportunity to play. Brandon enjoyed his experience and was determined to improve his abilities by practicing with his father which resulted in his being selected as most valuable teammate. Chris quickly lost interest in practicing and even though his father would not allow him to quit the team, once the season was over Chris was done with participating in organized sports.

The elementary school years emphasize adjustment, processing, and application of information. Children who are self-assured and comfortable with taking on challenges generally achieve according to their intellectual ability. If their effort is encouraged and supported by caregivers, they embrace the learning process and strive to be successful. Children with reduced self-confidence and those who lack emotional support are likely to achieve at lower levels than their intellectual ability. Excessive criticism for performance diminishes their motivation resulting in frustration and underachievement.

In the workplace, confident employees seek opportunities for enhancement. They embrace continuing education, seek new challenges, and benefit from mentoring by experienced staff. Constricted employees prefer the routine. They generally put in their time to collect their pay. They are likely to be interested in learning, but they may avoid opportunities for fear of failure.

Stage 5: Identity vs. Role Confusion

Brandon's successes, both academically and socially were linked to his parent's commitment to helping him learn from any experience he encountered. Their goal was to promote curiosity and understanding of personal and world events. Chris's struggles academically appeared to be rooted in his lack of effort and self-discipline. His father's emphasis on retaliation, judgement, and blame did little to encourage Chris to try to understand why he was struggling or how to make changes.

Adolescence features significant changes, both physically and emotionally. It is a period of self-definition, values clarification, and relationship development. A broader range of influences impacts the individual's sense of identity. Well-rounded, productive children experience adolescence as an opportunity to transition from familial dependence to their own definition of performance, social expectations, and future goals. Children who enter this period without a solid personality foundation frequently struggle with achievement and social relationships. Adolescents are generally attracted to those who think and act similarly to how they perceive themselves to be. Achievers seek to associate with achievers. And, likewise, underachievers tend to associate with other underachievers. Adolescents who lack a clear sense of identity often experience the future as anxiety-provoking and at extreme levels may become rebellious and non-conforming.

So, how does this apply to the workplace? Enhanced employees are productivity driven. They pursue a value-laden role with opportunities for advancement. They will focus on developing work goals that they believe will enhance their status and positively impact their future. Employees who are unsure of their value or purpose seek to avoid the limelight and may become disgruntled from feeling unappreciated. With few work goals, they often are passed over for promotion. They experience frustration at their lack of personal growth and change jobs frequently looking for the ideal job that will satisfy them. They fail to recognize how their mind-set contributes to their workplace frustration.

Stage 6: Intimacy vs. Isolation

Brandon's positive self-esteem and sense of identity were strong contributors to his relationship success. Chris, like his parents, would struggle with intimacy issues that eventually resulted in relationship breakups. Chris's lack of a strong relationship role model throughout his earlier stages left him unskilled in creating and maintaining a relationship in his own life. This also translates into working relationships and/or isolation as people of this age transition into the workplace.

Erikson viewed this period as critical in developing affiliations. Post-high-school-age individuals are considering work alternatives, career paths, and long-term relationships. There is a transition from self-centered thinking to an adaptation of shared responsibilities and expectations.

Those individuals with a clear sense of personal identity are equipped for success in educational, work, and social ventures. Individuals with a confused sense of identity may find it difficult to determine a path for their future, often shifting from situation to situation while looking for the right fit for them. They may find it difficult to establish and sustain meaningful relationships.

In the workplace, employees with a strong sense of self-esteem are generally effective in establishing meaningful relationships. They seek connections that will advance their careers. They seek collaborations where they can effectively engage with others to achieve a goal while maintaining their sense of individuality. Employees who lack confidence are likely to isolate themselves or seek the companionship of others with a similar perspective. There is potential for interpersonal conflict with those they view as overachievers or manipulators. They are more prone to blame others for their frustration.

Stage 7: Generativity vs. Stagnation

By far, the longest of the stages of development, adulthood can be experienced as opportunity for achievement or a perpetual struggle and everything in between. The personality characteristics developed in the earlier stages have considerable impact on the myriad of life experiences which occur over a period of forty-plus years. The impact of this stage on the work experience will be a focus as we consider generational differences. We can only speculate where Brandon's and Chris's lives would take them throughout this stage, but we would expect that the values and lessons learned (or not learned) through the previous stages would continue to be a part of their thought processes, decision-making abilities, and behaviors. Although Chris was not well-equipped by his parents, there could still be hope for him. Leaders in the workplace who understand levels of development can become mentors and role models for those who have not had the opportunity to have these skills developed in their own lives.

Thriving employees seek to be productive, upwardly mobile, and potential leaders. Often they flourish as mentors to new employees because of their productive attitude toward work and their company. They actively plan for meaningful retirement. Employees who feel stuck experience work as drudgery. If they remain at a job, it is likely to be a source of perpetual frustration. When they change jobs, they likely end up with the same unsatisfying work life.

Stage 8: Ego Integrity vs. Despair

The later years of life are a time for reflection, and as life expectancies have lengthened, they are an opportunity for further personal growth. The wisdom obtained through experience in the workplace may be cherished or considered irrelevant by subsequent generations as we will examine in the chapters ahead. Positive development through the earlier stages can make this stage a joyous and fulfilling time. Lack of previous development can turn these years into a time filled with stress and uncertainty.

Accomplished employees reflect on their successes and plan for a fulfilling retirement. Many look for opportunities to give back to society through volunteer work. They seek out places where they can continue to contribute. Frustrated employees stress over their retirement, feeling like they wasted the best years of their lives.

Experiences influence development. Human growth, personality formation, workplace productivity, and satisfaction are a developmental process. Understanding this process is key to structuring plans to help employees make productive adjustments to challenging situations. In the chapters that follow, we will present strategies for workplace enhancement that focus both on individual development and blending of generational similarities. Before moving on, let's consider an additional theory on human needs. In the stories that opened this book there were frequent references to basic safety and relational needs. Abraham Maslow's Hierarchy of Needs provides insight into how needs impact behavior and attitude.

MASLOW'S HIERARCHY OF NEEDS

In his 1943 paper "A Theory of Human Motivation," Maslow theorized that human existence evolves from a foundation of need and experience. Maslow's hierarchy is generally depicted as a pyramid with a wide base and a narrow pinnacle. Progress to each level is based on the individual's ability to meet the needs at the level below.

Basic Needs Refer to Survival

Consider the determination of Thien Tran to create a sense of stability for his family and the impact it had on their development as he relocated them into a new world. Food, water, and shelter are the basic needs for existence. Individuals struggling to meet their basic needs focus their attention on acquiring what they need to survive. The greater the effort to meet basic needs, the greater appreciation for the effort to obtain them.

Safety Needs

This refers to the individual's need for protection and security. When basic needs are being met, attention turns to creating a stable life experience. The human condition is fraught with vulnerability. There is a need to protect against the threat of vulnerability which produces motivation to increase the individual's sense of safety and security. Threats that are imminent receive primary attention. Threats that are perceived are given secondary attention. The greater the effort put into obtaining safety and security, the greater the appreciation for the importance of establishing systems to provide for safety needs. In our story, both families in the story were challenged by the 911 attack on the United States. The Martins reacted with outrage and a desire for retaliation. The Tran family chose to process the events with their son and determine how the experience could be productive in shaping his future.

Love and Belongingness

By nature, human beings are social creatures that seek affiliation. Human existence depends on caregiving and nurturing of others to meet their basic needs. Humans have a natural desire to assimilate into larger groups for protection and to establish a feeling of connectedness. When basic and safety needs are met, individuals seek to establish emotional connections. As emotional connections intensify, close personal bonds form creating feelings of love and belongingness.

In the story, we see important relationships develop when a family's dog destroys the neighbors' flowerbed. That connection extended to the next generation as we saw in Brandon and Chris's friendship. We also see how the continuation of love and connectedness demonstrated by Brandon's parents and grandparents framed his confidence and sense of inclusion—traits he carried with him into the business world.

Esteem

All of us seek validation of our value from others. We desire attention and affirmation of our worth from those we value. When we feel safe, secure, valued, and loved, we experience a sense of self-worth. Furthermore, we seek accomplishment and respect to validate our importance to others. We desire to be recognized as significant for whom we are or for the contributions we make. In our story, Brandon's development resulted in his success and validation by others both as a child (as best teammate) and later in work and relationships. Chris, on the other hand, struggled with his personal sense of esteem which hindered his success in both business and personal scenarios.

Actualization

Self-actualization is the desire to reach one's full potential, to find a sense of self-validation that is beyond being esteemed by others.

The theories of Erikson and Maslow emphasize the significance of foundation in human personality development. Success adjusting at each stage enhances the individual's ability to function at the next phase. Less productive adjustment at each stage detracts or alters the individual's ability to adjust at subsequent stages. Individuals who enter the workplace bring both unique personal characteristics along with generational commonalities. Both aspects contribute to successes and struggles. Many struggles can be overcome when the person understands what about them is contributing to the struggle. Let's return to the story to illustrate this concept.

Brandon's and Chris's lives couldn't have been more different. Brandon continued to find success in space and rocketry. He and his wife Sara bought a two-story house in the influential Houston, Texas, suburb of Sugar Land. He became a desired public speaker on space sciences. It was through this that Chris found his old friend.

Chris was laid off when the house that had been converted into the recording studio where he worked was sold to make room for housing in 2018. He rented a small apartment in the Antioch section of Nashville and began to think about where he was going in his life. He was watching *Good Morning America* one Thursday morning when Brandon Tran was introduced as the next guest. Chris's eyes lit up as he watched his childhood friend's introduction. They soon filled with tears as he compared his life situation to that of Brandon's.

The following week, when Brandon returned to his office in Houston, he found an unexpected e-mail in his inbox:

Hi, Brandon . . . Its Chris Martin. I saw you on GMA this morning. I am so proud of what you have become. I myself have pretty much struggled in life. It's crazy how two kids could grow up pretty much doing everything together and yet turn out so differently. I really thought I was doing the right thing by coming to Nashville to do the sound engineering gig. My mom and dad told me that I should just do what I liked. I don't know if you have heard or not, but they split up earlier this year. I got divorced a few years ago.

I could really use your help, Brandon. I need someone to talk to. I know now that I wasted a lot of my life "playing" instead of becoming prepared like you did. Do you think it's too late for me? Anyway, I would love to hear from you. Any advice you can give me will be greatly appreciated.

Your old friend, Chris

Brandon sat back in his chair, took another sip of his coffee, and closed his eyes. His heart broke for his friend. He thought back to some of the things he recalled from childhood. In retrospect, he could see the differences in the way they were each raised. He silently thanked his parents for equipping him for success. He felt a deep sense of empathy for his friend's position. The servant leader in him came out as he drafted the return email.

Hi Chris,

It's good to hear from you. I often wondered what happened to you and your family. I am sorry that things haven't turned out the way you would have hoped. The good news is that it is never too late to start down the road to success. There are lots of situations where people failed over and over before they finally got things figured out. We are still young. You have your whole life ahead of you. It will, however, require you to rethink some of the values that you have absorbed in your life. Sometimes it's not easy to do that, but I think you have a strong enough will to make it happen.

I checked with my wife Sara and would like to make an offer to you. We have plenty of room here in Houston. Would you consider coming down here and staying with us for a little while? I think being in a positive home would do you some good. I also have a friend who owns a growing cloud-based data storage business. He has a strong professional development program. They focus a lot on the soft skill and personality items that make people successful. I am pretty sure I can get you a position with him. If you are willing to learn, he can help you get some of the things you missed out on earlier in life. I know starting over isn't easy, but like I said, it's never too late. Let me know if you are interested. I will make all of the necessary arrangements.

Your friend always,
Brandon

CHAPTER 7

Framing a New-world Workplace

My mother texted me, "What do IDK, LY, and TTYL mean?"
I answered, "I don't know, love you, talk to you later."
She replied, "OK, I'll ask your sister."

So far on our journey of understanding the challenges of the multigenerational workplace, we have learned a few things about people that can influence how generations come together. We have discovered that:

- People think, act, and make decisions based on all of the things that have happened to (influenced and/or impacted) them throughout their lives. Each of us is a product of all of the things we have experienced up to this very minute.
- People form patterns of behavior based on what has worked for them or not worked for them in the past.
- People tend to think and act based on their own perspectives. Since these are drawn from their own experiences, they are more easily adopted than alternative paths.

- People often dismiss other points of view instead of embracing the good that might be found in open-mindedness.
- People with more experience often feel that their knowledge gained has more value than what those with less experience bring to the table.

While these things might make us feel "in control" of our environment, they are not always the best course of action for creating unity and harmony among different generations. In the previous chapter, we learned how to become more open-minded regarding learning how to embrace other's ideas, opinions, and viewpoints.

In this chapter, we will look at seven proven changes that can be implemented in any workplace to bring the generations together for harmony and productivity. Each of these will be looked at from three perspectives.

- Understanding the challenge
- Creating the plan
- Why it is important to your workplace

It is important to note here that these study areas are not unique to our work. We are striving to present them in a manner that makes them easy to understand and simple to implement. Many successful companies like General Electric, Deloitte, Google, Adobe, Microsoft, and Apple objectively use programs similar to these in order to create a more productive workplace. Progress requires change, adaptation, and maybe a little compromise—or, worse yet, sacrifice. The topics we discuss are suggestions of how to create a new-world workplace in any company. Your particular company might find some of them useful and others not so useful. You might also realize the possibilities and develop your own variations. The important thing is that you learn from the topics and open your minds to possibilities. If you are of an older generation, you might need to change the way you have always thought of your workplace culture. If you are of a younger generation, you might think of how you can influence your workplace culture from a new perspective. Regardless of your age, title, or tenure, you have the ability to positively influence your workplace. It doesn't matter where the application ideas come from, only that we learn to see the culture through new lenses. The objective is to create a workplace where everyone can be their best. Creating that new-world workplace is more important than the path you take to get there.

Let's get started.

Communication:
The Fundamental Competency

Understanding the Challenge: "Generations communicate differently"

In order to understand how we can learn to communicate effectively, we need to fully understand what communication is. There are three things required for communication: a sender, a receiver, and a message. This model can be verbal (talking to one another), non-verbal (body language or gestures), written (encompassing numerous platforms), symbolic (emojis), hieroglyphics, or a whole host of other methods of getting a message to another. What is important, regardless of the style used, is that the message sent equals the message received. If that doesn't occur, communication has not been achieved. When "what I said" does not equal "what you heard" there is confusion. Confusion in communication creates chaos instead of harmony in the workplace. Simple things like presuming understanding, communicating with word choices that are created by a group of people and seem like a second language to them, and using colloquial slang can generate barriers to effective communication. Likewise, if the method of communication doesn't resonate with the receiver, there is a risk that the overall message might not be conveyed.

When we look at the generations that are present in the workplace today, we need to understand what has influenced each generation in the style of communication that they prefer. The traditionalists got their input from talking to others, reading publications like newspapers and magazines, and listening to the radio. They learned to communicate very directly, literally, and simply. They learned by listening and reading. When FDR gave a fireside chat, everyone sat around the radio and listened intently. After the broadcast (intake of information) was completed, face-to-face conversation debated and clarified the message sent. Opinions were swayed, stands were taken, and personal bonds were either strengthened or damaged.

The baby boomers came of age along with commercial television. While they still did a lot of reading (textbooks, magazines, encyclopedias, etc.), they also were influenced by the visual input from television. Younger generations need to understand that television was not like today's broadband delivery of infinite choices. Most baby boomers only had access to a small number of channels. The local and national news broadcasts were how they learned what was going on in the world. They learned from seeing. The information gathered visually helped form their opinions and viewpoints. Watching the civil rights struggles and the anti-Vietnam war protests sent a strong message. Many became more nationalistic and moved to support the country's efforts. Others turned towards rebellion and took a stand against what they felt was morally wrong. They learned to become opinionated and to speak strongly from their passion.

As technology progressed, the Generation Xers were provided with early computers and video games. Remember, however, that this was pre-internet. The popular phrase for what you could do on a computer was known as "garbage in, garbage out." This meant that you could only get out of your stand-alone system what you had loaded into it. Software and applications were not anywhere near the range of what is available today. Video games were very simplistic compared to today's offerings. Both required a level of hand-eye coordination in order to master skills that would lead to technological competency. During this time, additional new business tools like voicemail and personal data recorders also became popular. Gen Xers learned to interact and communicate both visually and kinesthetically. Because they needed to take physical actions to generate a lot of their communication, they learned to be very linear and checklist driven. Generation Xers are more comfortable communicating across numerous platforms but still prefer to be direct.

The millennial generation came of age during a time of advancing technology. The internet has made access to information easy. Google and Siri replaced the massive volumes of encyclopedias that were once the standard of reference. Such a wealth of information in a single source made communication less interactive and more individual. The rise of digital social media created a comfortable platform for millennials to extend themselves to relationships formed through text messages and emojis. Since they learned more individually, communication via digital platforms became their comfort zone. In addition, education shifted to more group engagement than individual performance. People in the millennial generation learned that there was a level of comfort in small groups. One-on-one direct communication is not a desired part of their style.

As you can see, if each generation remains in the style of communication with which they became comfortable, we will have little communication at all. Learning how to accept and embrace the style most preferred by other generations is the beginning of harmony in the workplace.

Creating the Plan: "What we can do about it"

Knowledge is the beginning of understanding. First and foremost, all generations need to open their minds to understand the style of those with whom they are communicating. Baby boomers will generally not be receptive to text abbreviations, and a hard copy memo will not have much impact on a millennial. Every communication option available to us has its benefits and merits. Being receptive to learning the advantages of every style will create a more well-rounded communication system in any business. The key to getting past the barriers is first establishing a cadence for communication. Setting aside specific time for more in-depth talks is a must. Hopefully, ease of communicating in the workplace will become standard.

Leaders need to open their doors to at least two hours per month of one-on-one time with their direct reports. It is important that they first ask their people where and how they would like to meet. These sessions should not be directed by the leader. Leaders need to let their people know that this is time set aside in their day to talk about whatever is important to the employee. At least one session should be focused on the employee's personal professional development. We will have more on that later. One of the first things that should be discussed is how each of them would prefer to communicate on a daily basis. Baby boomers might learn that their millennial team member wants to get text messages. A Generation Xer might want to only see emails. A baby boomer could ask for people to come talk face-to-face. The important thing here is that channels for quality communication are opening. Remember that baby boomers tend to look to the needs of the business first and will act directly to achieve results. Generation Xers are very process-oriented and tend to think of results first. Millennials have a need to understand the "why" of things they are asked to do. Older generation leaders must take the time to explain the "why" to them and help them understand how their actions fit into the overall mission of the team and the business. Younger generation leaders need to be more direct and succinct in providing work direction to an older workforce. In all cases, leaders need to listen first with the intent to understand. In order to have quality communication, everyone must have common frames of reference speak a language (verbal and/or written) that everyone understands.

Another important key to establishing great communication in the workplace is "getting the noise out." Let's examine what is meant by noise in the workplace. Examples of "business noise" include discourse, arguing, whining and complaining, gossiping, and dissention. These things are the opposite of harmony, and that is what we need to create in our workplaces in order for everyone, from all generations, to do their best. Create open forums for people to be heard. It doesn't mean that you have to act on everything, but people need to be able to have a voice. An example of this might be leaders meeting in focus groups with another leader's team. Make sure that everyone knows coming in that it is a place where they can be heard in confidence. Information gathered should be studied anonymously to protect the speaker(s). It only takes one breach of trust to cause the entire plan to disintegrate. Another way to get the noise out is to think about how work direction is provided. Initially, for new people, that still needs to be highly directive. But for more seasoned folks, it should be more collaborative instead of delegating. Instead of saying, "I need you to do this," you might say, "This is what we need to achieve. What ideas do you have on how we can most easily accomplish this?" Get creative. You will be amazed what ideas arise when you open your mind to doing things differently. It is important to remember however that success can look different to people of other generations. Where achieving goals might be the picture of success for a baby boomer or Gen Xer, a millennial might be more focused on the pathway to get there or how their work impacts society.

Why is this important? What will it mean to your business?

People who are communicating effectively and in a timely manner create a sense of ease in the business that increases engagement and productivity. When people stop spending their time creating "noise," they focus more on collaboration. An environment of creativity and progress is fostered. People look for ways to work together, and this fits right into one of the desires of the way those in the millennial generation like to work. People begin helping each other learn and grow. And that impacts the business overall. People start to miss less time because they look forward to engaging with their peers. And, people who feel better about their work environment and their leaders are less likely to leave their job for a different workplace. Once we create a work culture of open, clear, and continual effective communication, we open the door for generations to come together with harmony and increased productivity.

Minimize the Hierarchy:
Create a New Work Environment

Understanding the Challenge: The Corporate Ladder No Longer Exists

There was a day when businesses were structured in traditional layers. Entry-level meant "starting at the bottom." In today's workplace, many entry-level people are on-boarded, bringing intense and diverse skills. They are strong contributors right out of the gate. In the old workplace, ranks and levels were defined and were looked at as levels of promotion. If you worked hard and contributed beyond expectations, you could move up to the next level. The advent of video gaming changed all of that. In video gaming, players learn that they can "level up" independently and that their skills grow along with that feeling of advancement. It is not just dependent on how long you play the game but what you accomplish in the game. They also learn that the skills required to "level up" are diverse and obtained through a myriad of experiences. The same holds true in the business world. As people learn that they have more control over the value they bring to the table, they expect to be more engaged in additional areas of planning and contributing. Leaders begin to realize that people bring more great ideas than they had ever expected. The idea that only C-suite and/or senior management are capable of understanding the vision begins to disintegrate. Millennial employees see the old structure as archaic, and they want to be included in information transfer at all levels. Layers in the workplace suppress communication. Senior managers begin to feel like they have all of the power. Lower levels feel like worker ants, carrying out the desires of those in power. Layers also suppress collaboration and diminish the feeling of individual ownership.

In a well-structured business today, multiple channels of growth opportunities exist that capitalize on similar skills. An example of this is that leadership requires competency in skill sets that are similar, regardless of the area of the business. Creating learning opportunities for people in a general path versus a specific department or work area removes the stigma of hierarchal structure. Layers also suppress trust. When direction is strictly top-down, people don't feel valued or appreciated. When they feel that they are respected as having input to the organization, the sense of inclusion motivates them to be even stronger contributors. Many businesses still implement change management in a traditional manner. Senior leadership creates a team to study the situation and then decides how the change will be implemented. In most cases, each level of hierarchy rolls the change down to those below their level. By the time it gets to individual contributors, it is purely directional; they don't feel like they have any input in the decision. Layers foster favoritism and disparate treatment. Individual contributors will still see senior management as "the ivory tower" and that their ideas and feeling about the workplace don't matter. Each of these challenges not only leads to lower productivity but contribute strongly to employee attrition. Senior leaders who realize they have many nontraditional avenues for how their workplace is structured create a culture of communication and growth. And people who feel connected are much more apt to continue to seek opportunities to be even stronger contributors.

Creating the Plan: "What we can do about it"

When we say "minimize the hierarchy," we do not mean that businesses need to eliminate roles or titles. Businesses should, however, analyze their organizational charts and decide if the structure truly represents what positions they need to achieve their goals and objectives. It might be that similar roles and/or titles can be combined into a single work unit. Being cognizant of the structural layers within your business is the first step to ensuring that active communication is being implemented with the inclusion of all levels. The important thing is that you seek ways to encompass all levels and generations according to their expertise in how the business progresses.

Leaders need to learn how to collaborate. Unfortunately, the word "collaboration" is so overused and overhyped that it has become meaningless. We talk about collaborative software, but, in reality, technology cannot replace true collaboration. It can, however, make it easier and more efficient. Real collaboration is two or more people working together toward a shared goal. You can see how much effective communication plays into this principle. Although technology is a great tool for workflow, collaboration truly exists between people. Older generations need to learn that it is OK to use technology as a collaborative tool and let younger generations know that they see the value in it. Everyone in the workplace, regardless of job title or generation, needs to find ways to effectively work together with others. Look for ways to collaborate whenever you see the need to delegate. It might be a more effective tool to achieve the goal. Being open to effective collaboration ensures that the doors that lead to new vision are not closed. Closed doors can create division, and division can be a cancer in the workplace. It can create a perception of favoritism. At the very least, it contributes to disunion. We have all seen business gatherings where the finance people, the operations folks, the IT team, and leadership all gravitate to their own little groups for seating. Fostering a culture of collaboration will reduce that separatism and will get the creative conversations moving in the right direction. Make it a point to emphasize the importance of collaboration at all business gatherings.

Instead of top-down directive change management, explore the organizational development concept of appreciative inquiry. Appreciative inquiry, according to Wikipedia, is "a model that seeks to engage stakeholders in self-determined change."[3] It was developed at Case Western Reserve University in 1987. Appreciative inquiry looks to find the best

---

[3] Appreciative Inquiry, Wikipedia, https://en.wikipedia.org/wiki/Appreciative_inquiry.

of what is currently in place in order to determine what could be. Instead of asking "What is wrong?" we should ask "What is working well?" and build on that in order to create effective change. Including all levels and generations in this inquiry will build trust and confidence with your entire work force, leading to harmony and stronger engagement.

Have leaders focus on being engaged with people beyond their direct reports. This opens pathways for all levels and generations to have their voice heard by more than a single person. Create multigenerational focus groups to provide a safe environment for generations to come together and learn from each other. Facilitate these sessions to ensure that everyone has equal opportunity to provide input and that no one's input is diminished or belittled. This is sometimes hard to do across generations, but a strong session leader will have no problem keeping the energy positive. Likewise, have leaders, regardless of their generation; purposefully take time to talk with people from other generations. Encourage people from younger generations to communicate with leaders from older generations. Make sure that all leaders, regardless of their generation, keep the doors of communication open at all times. This will not only provide surprising good input, but it will also make that person feel valued and appreciated. Most importantly, businesses must learn to include valuable people in all levels of communication to ensure that they are capitalizing on the value that all generations bring to the operation. Learn to have a mind-set of including a variety of people instead of creating traditional closed work groups.

Why is this important? What will it mean to your business?

Business thrives when everyone feels a connection to the mission. Allowing all generations to provide their input and viewpoint will help create an environment for effective communication. Minimizing hierarchy, whether organizationally or in communication, is the beginning of bringing people together. People who feel like leaders are listening will be more engaged and productive. Being cognizant of peoples' values, competencies, and generational perspectives will help you to retain key talent within your organization. It will also create stronger channels for professional growth. Those opportunities will be more transparent within your business, and upward moves within the organization will become more obvious. It will create a "you push me, and I will pull you" culture. An environment with less layered structure and more opportunities for people of all levels to communicate openly is the beginning of cross-generational learning. And, most importantly, it promotes ownership of individual behaviors.

Promote Individual Development: Watch Them Grow or Watch Them Go

Understanding the Challenge: It's More than a Job Description

As we have seen earlier, baby boomers, Generation Xers, and millennials have all experienced learning differently. Also, we have seen that the workplace looked very different as each generation became a part of it. Baby boomers and Generation Xers were part of a more traditional workplace prior to the advent of increased technology. The tech changes that have happened since then have totally reshaped the workplace. In the same manner, baby boomers and Generation Xers had a clearer vision of what the workplace would look like as they were preparing to become a part of it. Higher education degrees better prepared those generations for the skills and competencies they would need to be successful. Technology is advancing at a rate that none of us would have ever believed possible.

Millennials are the children of baby boomers and older Gen X parents. As they were coming of age, their parents encouraged them to follow the higher education pathway that had been successful for them. Parents told their millennial children, "Get a college education and everything will work out OK." Unfortunately, that isn't going exactly as planned. The millennial generation entered the workforce with huge college debt challenges and jobs that often didn't provide enough to make those debt payments. That generation, however, became conditioned to believe that learning and growing equals success. They carry the need to learn into the workplace with them. Continuing to develop professionally has become a basic part of their work/life balance. Statistics show that millennials tend to leave their current work employer within three years if they don't feel they are getting opportunities to learn and grow.[4] Businesses are continuing to grow and change. Advancing technology in the areas of robotics and artificial intelligence is creating new roles and positions every day. Many businesses don't have adequate bench strength to fill these new roles as they become a reality. Likewise, many businesses don't have succession plans in place to backfill key existing roles in their workforce. Traditional pipelines to fill these roles no longer work. The old corporate ladder model of advancement where leaders taught those in their department the nuances of their position thereby preparing them for that vertical promotion are outdated. Over 30 percent of leaders are placed in newly created roles annually.[5] Similarly, the traditional ways of identifying high-potential talent in businesses is also archaic. Gone are the days where recommendations based on high performance were key indicators of high-potential talent. The new workplace needs objective criteria for identifying those who truly have potential to become tomorrow's leaders. As businesses streamline their operations, fewer next-level roles are available. Nearly three-quarters of successor candidates do not perceive significant opportunity for career progression within their organizations.[6] Finally, the measurement of potential talent in organizations is no longer based on seniority. As we have seen, new talent, especially in the millennial generation, brings marketable knowledge to business immediately upon hire. Updated skills and competence within major disciplines is becoming more of the norm than job descriptions and associated tasks as a measure of advancement.

All generations, and especially millennials, feel the need to learn and

---

[4] SkillDirector, "Why Employees Taking Charge of Their Learning Is Good for You," July 6, 2016, https://skilldirector.com/news/employees-take-charge-of-learning.

[5] Shaurav Sen, "Succession Strategies for the New Work Environment," CEB, December 12, 2014, http://www.assessmentanalytics.com/wp-content/uploads/2014/12/CEB-Succession-Planning-Presentation-Deck.pdf.

[6] Ibid.

grow specific to their roles and career paths. Not providing the opportunity for this often leads to employee attrition. And, of course, this comes at a cost. First, there needs to be some mechanism in place to refill the role. Traditional sourcing and onboarding is very expensive for any role. Additionally, there may be the inability to provide contractual service levels, potential client relations challenges, added stress to remaining team members who need to pick up the work left by the departing person, and strained internal relations. All of these add additional hidden costs to employee turnover.

Lastly, many current leaders are not prepared to develop people nontraditionally. To many older generation leaders, professional development means taking classes, getting an additional degree, attending a conference, or reading a book. Few of these adequately provide for the specific needs of the workplace. Nontraditional, on-the-job learning channels provide opportunities for people to gain the skills specific to the business in which they want to advance. Nontraditional business learning opportunities not only better prepare people for future roles but also keep them more engaged and increase productivity while they are learning. All of this leads to reduced attrition.

Creating the Plan: "What we can do about it"

As we've already mentioned, traditional methods of identifying high-potential talent are no longer effective. Objective criteria selection not only provides more accurate candidate selection but also shields businesses from potential disparate treatment within their workforce. High-potential selection criteria need to be transparent throughout the business. Everyone should know that the program exists and what the process is to apply for inclusion. Details of the application, selection process, and the development plan needs to be clearly communicated to all. Companies that have implemented successful succession programs have found that there are three areas that predictably generate stronger candidates. These three areas are:

- High aspiration: Will they get there?
- High ability: Will they be effective?
- High engagement: Will they remain with your company?

Having an effective and objective selection process that identifies those people who meet all three criteria leads the business to a successful high-potential development program. Successful high-potential development programs create strong bench strength for key roles within the business. And, having the right staff to be prepared for the future saves the business money.

One size seldom fits all. The same is true with individual development plans. Each of us, as unique individuals, has become a product of everything we have experienced up till today. We all have distinctive strengths, values, and ethics. We also each have a different vision of where we want our futures to lead. Individual development plans are designed to identify where we are as a building block for creating our professional future. While the actual forms used to track skill growth may vary, the program itself needs to have similar components.

1. Begin with conversations between the employee and the leader to identify where the employee wants to go professionally. Sometimes it helps to first identify what they want to achieve in their personal life ("What do you see your life looking like in the year 2025?"). It is usually easier for people to picture having a boat, traveling, having a family, etc. Once they begin seeing their future life, transitioning to what they need to accomplish professionally in order to achieve it becomes easier.
2. Identify strengths and build on them.
3. Identify opportunities for growth in their current role. How can they get better at what they are doing now? What skills would help them achieve beyond expectations?

4. Create a plan to gain competence in the identified skills. Where in the business can they gain knowledge of the skill(s) and put their learning into practice? How will they demonstrate that they have achieved mastery? What will be the target date to become competent?

5. The most important style of leadership here is the "connector leader." Not every direct leader has depth in areas that might have been identified as growth opportunities. A good connector leader seeks the best available person to help people learn, develop, and master skills. They connect the person being developed to the best source of influence. In this way, people are learning from the true subject matter experts, and a high-level mastery is achieved.

6. After they have mastered skills that pertain to their current role, move to identifying skills that they will need in their future role. Follow the same process for skill mastery and demonstrated competence.

Some important things to remember are:

- Don't get in a hurry. Numerous quality conversations are required to properly diagnose and create a great plan.
- Help the employee self-discover as much as possible. Leaders should do a lot of listening and asking questions to help the employee clarify their thoughts.
- Document all plans on a form that will allow you to track progress and define mastery.
- Don't work on more than two skills at one time. As skills are mastered, add new ones to keep the development moving forward.
- Individuals are responsible for their own development (the actions taken to learn new skills); leaders are responsible only

for providing direction and support, helping to identify learning opportunities, and attesting to competence.

As your talent bench grows in strength, the next logical step is to discover how to best utilize the new talent you are developing. Highly successful businesses realize that succession planning is the key to doing that. Businesses generally have formal strategic visions that lead them to achieving their business goals. Progressive companies marry their talent development programs with their strategic vision. Talent needs are identified at the same time that the plans to move forward are implemented. Key talent from the high-potential pool is identified and targeted for required positions. Individual development becomes more strategic with these people to best prepare them to seamlessly step into new roles. It is important to remember to keep that development focused on skills and competence instead of job descriptions and associated tasks. Look to job descriptions and the associated functions of that position to determine what key skills are necessary to perform those functions. Always define the required actions of a position in terms of the skills required to make someone highly successful in that new role.

One of the key pieces of executing a strong talent development program involves understanding nontraditional learning opportunities. As we mentioned earlier, these are ways that people can learn and master skills within the business. Keeping the learning internal increases their visibility within the organization, increases their personal level of engagement, and improves the likelihood of you keeping them. Nontraditional learning opportunities within the business includes (but is not limited to) things like mentoring, temporary job assignments, and special project work. Including people in areas that are not normally a part of their role expands their horizons. As leaders identify those nontraditional learning opportunities that lead to skill mastery, they should collect them in a shared location. This makes it easy for other leaders to have a quick reference for proven opportunities for people they are developing.

Why is this important? What will it mean to your business?

Many businesses have comprehensive benefit plans used to attract and retain employees. Many also have great rewards and recognition programs as well. Even though these kinds of programs are highly appreciated, nothing says "we care" like taking a personal interest in individuals. Individual professional development provides employees with transferrable and marketable skills that they can implement in their current role to perform at a higher level. They can also take these skills with them throughout their career. A feeling of loyalty is created with the business who takes this interest in them unlike any other benefit or reward program. Highly engaged employees become promoters of the business. They usually share their experiences with others which can lead to a "best place to work" reputation. This, in turn, helps to attract and retain other talent. Everyone is a winner. It creates bench strength that helps to prevent gaps in the business should external opportunities open for current employees. While most leaders are highly competent in the skills required to perform their assigned job functions, developing others requires skills that are not common to many roles. Many leaders are not competent in this area. Learning how to develop others adds an additional important skill talent to your leaders. Everyone grows! It opens new channels for communication and connects leaders to the business. Having a true staffing vision that accompanies your business's strategic growth vision will set the stage for continued progress, productivity, and true succession planning. Strong professional development leaders provide a network for better communication across all generations and help your business create harmony and productivity.

What was once seen as "the corporate ladder," purely vertical growth within a department or field, has become "the corporate climbing wall." Necessary skill sets are far more diverse. These skills are no longer learned in the traditional linear approach. There are opportunities for development in all areas of business. Business leaders who have a cognitive vision of where the best learning opportunities lie within their business regardless of the department or area see broader and deeper skill growth with their people. It changes the motivation from "what I need" to "what I want." When the business grows a diversified, supported, and driven culture from the top leaders down, it creates a thriving food chain of harmony, stability, and productivity.

Cross-mentor/Share knowledge: Everyone's a Learner and Everyone's a Teacher

Understanding the challenge: Everyone's Experiences Bring Value

Mentoring is one of the most misunderstood actions in the business world. To truly understand the challenge, we need to look at what mentoring really is, and what it isn't. Mentoring is a development tool. It is a process that allows people of all generations to grow skills in others, regardless of their age or tenure. It allows information and ideas to flow throughout the organization. It helps younger generations understand the business's operation, culture, and policies. It opens the eyes of older generations to new technology. In its fundamental form, it allows anyone to help everyone else grow within their area of expertise. In today's generationally diverse workplace, everyone has skills to share, and everyone has skills to learn. Mentoring is not "I can help you because I am older, wiser, and have been here longer." Mentoring is "Here are lessons I have learned about mastering this through my experience. I have learned these from both positive and negative outcomes. These are things you can't learn in a textbook."

We used to think of mentoring as Plato sitting at the feet of Socrates and gleaning life lessons from his learning and experience. While that might have been the model in ancient times, it no longer fits today's progressive business world. Today we realize that while the baby boomers and Generation Xers have a lot of experience and can help millennials and Gen Zers with relationship-building and company culture, the millennials and Gen Zers can teach their older coworkers how to more easily utilize the tools they already possess. Another misconception of mentoring is that it is general. Assigning a younger high-potential candidate to a senior director mentor because that director has had a successful career is not true mentoring. Real mentoring is very skill specific. It would be proper to assign a less experienced person to be a mentee with the same senior director if the skills needed were things like time management, establishing a personal brand, executive presentation, or presenting complex proposals (assuming that the senior director was an expert in that area). Not taking the time to determine who can best help people gain knowledge and competence in their specific areas of need is an error many businesses still make.

As businesses grow and become more complex, work groups tend to segregate, each focusing on their effort to bring value to the business. This tends to create invisible walls that keep key associated skills confined within that area. High-potential people can have a difficult time knowing where their opportunities lie in finding a viable mentor. This can drastically limit the scope of learning unless there is a mechanism to truly know what skills are needed to be competent in each of the isolated areas.

Lastly, it is important for us to bring out the danger of not using cross-mentoring. Imagine, if you will, a restaurant that never changes their menu offering. Day after day, the cooks come in and do exactly the same preparation processes with exactly the same dinner choices. How long will it take before they become bored with their work and the quality of food suffers? Additionally, day after day people come and order from the same limited menu options. How long will it take before they say, "I have eaten there before. Let's try something new?" Both of these situations are the result of simply not having someone with a greater depth or breadth of experience creating the plan. The menu might not need to change much, but the new techniques implemented would add a level of creativity and motivation to those cooking the meals. The less experienced cook might also have a technique or process that the more experienced chef had never seen. Every person helps another grow, regardless of how long they have been in the kitchen. It would also create newfound excitement for the diners. They would gladly go back to see what new twists were being added to menu items that they already knew they liked. The same thing happens in businesses every day. The lack of skilled people sharing what they have learned with others may cause the same level of stagnation and discouragement.

Creating the Plan: "What we can do about it"

The first thing we need to understand is that not everyone has natural mentoring skills. Many people are true subject matter experts in their field but have never had much experience in mentoring others. Developing others requires a completely different set of skills. Second, it can be very hard for leaders to let go of their preconceived notions about how we have traditionally defined mentoring. We need to reframe our understanding of mentoring and realize that it isn't as complicated as we might have thought. A quality mentor is a(n):

- Advisor – They act as a sounding board and facilitator. They recommend learning activities that will develop the desired skill(s) in the mentee.
- Developer – They provide guidance based on the knowledge they have learned through their experience. They provide direction and purpose. They empower the mentee.
- Coach – They challenge the mentee to learn and apply new things. They provide feedback to push the mentee to higher levels.
- Affirmer – They are understanding and enhance self-esteem. The praise the mentee for progress towards mastering the skill(s) and celebrate with them when they demonstrate competence.
- Sponsor – They provide the mentee visibility to others within the organization.

Businesses should create a simple but effective training program for people identified as viable mentors to help them ensure success through consistency. Many companies also provide a "cheat sheet" to help guide both the mentors and mentees through the process thereby helping both parties have a higher level of comfort and confidence.

It is also necessary for businesses to have a solid bank of mentors. These are people within the business who are highly competent in specific skill areas. Be sure to include people of all generations, especially the millennial generation, as they are usually the social technology experts. It just takes a little time to have potential mentors list the skill areas where they feel they have above-average strength. A few reference checks with others in the business will easily confirm that they are really strong in each area. Lists of potential mentors sorted by both mentor and skill area then becomes a quick reference tool for those seeking a mentor to master new skill areas. (A best practice in matching mentees with mentors, however, is to allow each person's leader to make the initial introduction.)

Another great way to match mentors with mentees is a "mentor meet and greet." An informal gathering (perhaps with refreshments) will keep things casual. Anyone seeking a mentor or desiring to be a mentor can attend. Name tags could be provided, but instead of saying "Hello, my name is . . .", they could say "Hello, my skill is . . ." If someone is looking for a mentor, their name tag could read, "Hello, I am seeking." When someone who is seeking a mentor sees a name tag with the skill they desire, an initial conversation can be easily generated around that area. It won't take long for names to be exchanged and a next-step meeting to be arranged to begin the mentoring process.

There should always be a feedback loop following a mentor arrangement. Part of the feedback should include the mentee describing the measure of success and how they demonstrated that to their mentor. This will be particularly important to the leader who is guiding that person's individual development plan. It is important that all mentees continually get the very best learning experiences. Providing feedback not only ensures success but it also ensures that mentors continue to grow stronger.

It is also important in mentoring to understand the difference between collaboration and cooperation. Both of these terms are often use synonymously in business, but they have very different meanings. Collaboration is when people work together to achieve the same goal, and it is more focused on sharing tools and/or resources. Sharing programs or applications on the internet or the company's intranet is a good example. Collaboration is a coordinated activity where people try to develop a solution shared between them. It is a collective activity. Each person's identity and skill growth are defined through the interactions between them. It is like a band playing together from the same sheet of music. Cooperation is also a process that allows people to work together toward achieving the same goal instead of competing. It has mutual benefit for all. Though the goal is the same, the perspective of each person may be different. Cooperation involves dividing the roles, tasks, or assignment with each person having their own responsibilities. It is a supportive activity where priority may or may not be with any one individual. It is like the band backing up a soloist. In effective mentoring, it is important that both people know when to be cooperative and when to be collaborative. Each has its place in the mentoring process, and both have great value when used at the correct time.

Why is this important? What will it mean to your business?

Mentoring fosters a culture of growth and development. It concentrates on each person's individual development needs and objectives based on their career and life aspirations. It mutually benefits both the mentee and the mentor, growing skill on both sides. It helps to build long-term relationships which helps retain talent. With effective mentoring programs, everyone gets stronger. It allows strength to improve weakness and weakness to improve strength. It improves the overall skill sets of the entire business which leads to greater productivity and results. It builds confidence in people that can lead to better personal and client relations. It also fosters a culture that includes both cooperation and collaboration and in doing so increases people's sense of value and self-worth.

For millennials, it will help them understand the culture of the business and feel a connection to what makes that business successful as well as understand the impact that success can have on society and the economy. Although they often come into a business with a perception different from older generations, millennials still must learn to adapt into cultures that may be different from any they have previously experienced. For baby boomers and Generation Xers, it will help them understand younger generations and move away from the mind-set of "I pay you to do a job. Why do I need to nurture you?" Many baby boomers are uncomfortable with social media sharing, cloud computing, and creating video as learning tools. Most millennials are experts in these areas. Allowing them to become mentors to the older people who would benefit from understanding their use provides the millennial generation with opportunities of importance.

Most importantly, cross-mentoring opens doors for building relationships that transcend generations. Better relationships help people discover a sense of belonging, caring, and inclusion. All of these contribute to creating a strong, harmonious, and productive workforce.

Be Flexible: Build Bridges out of Walls

Understanding the Challenge: Life Moves Faster than We Ever Expected

In order to fully understand the need for flexibility in the workplace, let's take a look back to the time of the traditionalist generation. When we met Walter earlier in the book, we learned a lot about how his world was shaped. We saw the structure of the workplace and the values that drove it. We learned how people like Walter formed their behaviors and lifestyle patterns. In order to go deeper into that work era, we also need to understand the common time frames of business.

For most people, whether blue-collar or white, the work week was Monday to Friday. Office hours began at 9:00 a.m. and went until 6:00 p.m. Lunch hour was generally from 12:00 noon until 1:00 p.m. Everyone came in together, went to lunch at the same time, and clocked out for the day at the same time. Even retail stores commonly closed at 6:00 p.m., allowing their employees to return home to spend time with their families. Stores open during any hours on Sunday were almost unheard of. Life was structured. The workplace was made up of mostly husbands; wives took care of the children, the shopping, and any other household requirements while their husbands were "on the job." Everyone understood that things would happen at the speed that communication allowed. Letters were stamped and placed in the care of the United States Post Office to be delivered in as much time as it took to get there. In most cases, communication could wait until the following business day. Lives were planned and structured. People accepted that structure and worked within that model.

Let's take a look at the millennial generation. Like we learned from Ashlee, the world in which millennials grew up was very different from those generations that went before them. The world is much more closely tied together through internet communication. The challenges of the world, both natural and political, are brought to the surface every hour of every day through on-demand news via the web. Millennials are more acutely tuned in to not only the needs of others but to the global efforts to assist or resist. They learned the value of social service from their baby boomer parents. Contributing to community service events became a modem for them to feel like they could give back and help improve the world around them. They also feel a need for personal time. Many millennials choose to engage in personal relationships later in life. Many don't start families until they are in their thirties. Most people in the millennial generation also get great value in experiencing new places and things instead of gathering personal possessions. Many put lifestyle ahead of work. Having time to Snapchat a special place or event that they are experiencing is a fundamental part of this generation. They didn't grow up in a well-structured lifestyle like Walter and Nancy did. As such, they don't work well in a workplace that has hourly confines.

Now let's look at today's busy world. Business and commerce happen every hour of the day, every day of the week and year. It doesn't even slow down, let alone take a break. People can buy anything they want at any time they want by accessing the internet. Business is no longer local. Many corporations have offices all over the world and expect their people to accommodate unstructured hours in order to keep it moving forward. E-mail and videoconferencing are used extensively at all hours of the day and night. The "all-in" need for availability wears on people and will eventually cause them to disengage.

This has brought on a complete change to the hours people are expected to work. Shifts are scheduled round the clock; leaders are expected to be available to support their teams whenever the need arises. Home life is expected to accommodate whatever is necessary to keep the business world running (e-mail all hours of the day and night on a smartphone). Add to that the pace at which new technology is created and implemented. IT teams work long nights in order to have new systems up and running the next day. Nontraditional learning is becoming the norm. People rush to learn how to use those new tools to get ahead of competition. The demand for flexibility creates the challenge for finding personal time to rest and unwind. People need flexibility in order to handle their personal lives. If business is going to demand that people be available at all hours in order to maintain continuity, it is only fair that business provides a mechanism for people to still escape to their personal space.

Creating the Plan: "What we can do about it"

As we learned earlier in this section, communication is the fundamental competency. Communicating openly and effectively is the beginning of building a flexible workplace where everyone from every generation can do their best. Flexibility in the workplace falls into two categories: workplace structure and hours of demand. We will look at each independently.

Can you imagine employees of the millennial generation being asked to dress in a business suit and report at exactly 9:00 a.m. as their traditionalist grandparents did? How much productivity would we see from these valuable people if they were forced to sit behind a desk in a closed-off office? The millennial generation has grown up in a world without structure and borders. They have come to expect the same thing in their workplace. Just about everyone now works from a portable computer. Gone are the cables and connections that held us in one place. The new workplace is one of openness and versatility. Companies that are getting the most productivity from their younger workforce realize that providing them with less structure dramatically increases their level of engagement. This versatility can be achieved in numerous ways. Here are some ideas:

- Begin with asking your workforce how they would like their work space to be configured. Today's workforce wants variety and opportunity in their space. Remember that while baby boomers and Generation Xers still have an appreciation for structure and self-discipline, millennials don't usually share those same values. They like a sense of freedom to decide the environment that best makes them feel engaged. Be open-minded. Look for easy places to begin. It is understandable that not every idea will be implementable. But just listening to ideas goes a long way to creating harmony in the workplace. It remains to be understood, however, that security and privacy are still factors that require varying levels of separation. Complying with these basic needs does not imply that leadership is closed-minded.

- Create a sense of openness in the work space. Don't confine millennial employees to a single desk. Make efforts to create open and inviting spaces. Cafés and lounges offering upscale coffees and teas create a relaxed and receptive place for people to collaborate and create. Look for ways to allow your workforce to engage from numerous locations within your offices. If you have outdoor and/or green spaces, be sure to have wireless capability strong enough to allow people to enjoy that green space whenever possible.

- Telecommuting (aka "working remote") is becoming a much more popular activity in recent years. It has benefits for the business in that it reduces the work space need and overhead. It is popular with the workforce because it saves commuting time, fuel, and preparation time. Businesses should do a deep analysis to determine the feasibility of allowing people to work from home. The demand for wildly varying hours created by global business makes this an attractive option for many people. Security matters can easily be resolved with the use of firewalls and VPN connections. Allowing people this flexibility builds loyalty, creates harmony, and increases engagement.

- Allow people to create their own work schedule. Not everyone is a "morning person." Many millennials keep different schedules than older generations. What is ultimately important is that outcomes and results are the highest priority to business. Allowing individuals to have input on the hours they work provides them with a sense of ownership over their work. This, in turn, leads to higher levels of quality and effectiveness. Older generations who both like and require more structure should still have the opportunity to be office bound and work the hours that best fits their lifestyle. This liberty, however, must come with restrictions. If the business has critical obligations that require people to be present in the office (critical meetings and/or internal or external client requirements) the people involved must still meet that "in the office" need. Additionally, leaders need to be made aware in advance and agree to people's plans to work flexibly.

- Community service is a more important part of the millennial's lifestyle than any previous generation. They were raised to understand that people have an obligation to give back to society. Social media has brought worldwide social issues to the forefront of their attention. They are acutely tuned in to the needs of those less privileged. They get a deep sense of reward in being a part of making the world a better place. It can sometimes be hard for baby boomers and Generation Xers to understand this sense of commitment. Again, an open mind to understanding this key area will go a long way in building harmony in the workplace. The balance between committed work hours and community service time requires a balance of understanding. Just as millennials feel the need to be active in community service, older generations have the same sense of caring that the business thrives. Putting business goals and objectives first is a part of their ingrained thinking. Businesses should try to accommodate those people in the workplace who feel the need to participate in community events. An understanding between the time away from work and the needs of the business need to be in balance. Business leaders should come to an agreement with those wanting to serve by agreeing to some key points.

- Any time requested to be absent for community service needs to be requested in advance enough for the business to be prepared.
- Clear delineation of the business requirements that need to be achieved prior to the time away needs to be understood by all parties.
- The time away will be approved as long as the predetermined business continuity plan has been achieved.
- Leadership will participate in the event(s) if at all possible based on business needs.

As we learned earlier, learning and growing on the job is an important part of everyone's (especially the millennial's) sense of professional well-being. We also learned that providing professional growth opportunities is a key way to bring generations together in the workplace. Among the nontraditional methods are:

- Job shadowing – Allow employees a day to follow along with an employee or leader in another area to learn what that job entails. This is a great opportunity to identify skills to be worked on within their individual development plan. It also will build relationships that lead to better communication and collaboration.
- Temporary job assignments – Like job shadowing, temporary assignments create exposure and bonds within

the business. With temporary assignments, however, the depth of skills built can lead to stronger bench strength throughout the business. Temporary assignments should be considered whenever the new assignment contributes to skill growth whenever those required skills cannot be learned within their current role. Although it might initially appear that they reduce effective business due to the learning curve in the new role, done correctly they will add value incrementally more than what is lost in initial learning.

Additionally, we need to reassess the way we look at performance goals and results. Flexibility is necessary in this area as well. Where the traditional structured workplace allowed for more static and predict-able results, the new-world workplace requires diversity and flexibil-ity. Businesses use more job descriptions now than ever. Goals and the required results are increasingly more individual as they relate to those positions. It is ever more important that performance is measured in terms of results and not activity. It becomes critical that we tie flexible goals (and the results) to flexibility in work hours. Businesses need to primarily focus their energy on meeting and exceeding company goals and objectives. How we get there is not as important as the accomplish-ment. Businesses need to allow people flexibility in creating a work schedule that benefits both the business and themselves, and thereby achieve their goals. The axiom of "that's how we do it because that is how we have always done it" needs to become nonexistent. When applied to the millennial generation, that rigid structure generally diminishes results. Think of it this way. If you have two people doing the work of a particular role and one produces 140 percent of the goal in thirty hours worked and the other one produces 110 percent of the goal in forty hours worked, which one has greater value to the business? Instead of criticiz-ing the overachiever for not working enough hours, we should praise that person for their effectiveness. There is nothing wrong with the second person's performance. However, comparing them to the first person will not create a positive outcome. Instead, we should be sharing the things that helped the first be more productive. Hours worked have nothing to do with that. If anything, we should be reevaluating to ensure that the goals are set correctly. Always focus on the outcomes and results and ensure that goals are set with enough flexibility to ensure success.

Why is this important? What will it mean to your business?

A work environment structured to provide maximum growth opportunities to everyone will be built on breaking down traditional walls of belief in how the business needs to be designed. In turn, it should build bridges that cross to all departments and people. In reality, people of all generations want flexibility in their professional lives. Baby boomers want time to go visit with grandchildren. Generation Xers desire to travel and experience exotic places. Millennials want time to spend with their children, have new life experiences, and provide community service. In a well-designed flexible workplace, everyone wins. The business also wins through increased engagement, productivity, and decreased employee turnover. It fosters an environment that is rich in creativity and professional growth. It also allows for more complex individual development which leads to a stronger succession plan. And most importantly, it shows everyone, from every generation, that the business truly cares about them.

Affinity Groups: Sharing Interest Promotes Engagement

Understanding the Challenge: We All Feel the Need to Be Connected

The need to be connected is a basic human trait. From the earliest times, people banded together for protection, assistance, and support. This is what led us to become civilized and to form communities. Today communities come in many different forms. We not only have the neighborhoods in which we live, but we have communities in our churches, civic organizations, and workplaces. The fast pace of our busy lifestyles, however, has caused many people to become disconnected. In recent years, we have seen the rise of digital media and online social applications replace the face-to-face human interactions. While these connections might be convenient, they cannot replace the emotional bonds we get from interacting personally with others. Digital connections provide a false and incomplete connection. In the new workplace we need to create convenient arenas for people to interact personally, not just digitally. All generations need this, and it is an especially helpful part of bringing generations together. This situation is particularly important to those individuals with identity issues that resent or seek to avoid interpersonal connections. The question is, "How do we find a common forum where people from diverse generations want to come together and interact?" The answer is, "Through affinity groups." Let's begin by defining affinity groups.

Affinity groups, also known as employee resource groups or network groups, are purposeful organizations within the workplace where people of all generations can come together based on shared characteristics or life experiences. These groups can be as diverse as the population of the business. Many affinity groups are formed around themes like gender, sexual orientation, ethnicity, or single parents. Others are formed around common interests like community service, wine enthusiasts, technology enthusiasts, foodies, or Harley riders.

One of the challenges that today's workplace has created is that work units tend to work individually, each contributing their piece to the overall business objectives. They are highly specialized units made up of highly talented people. Unfortunately, this leads to people primarily associating with those in their own area. We have all seen times when all of the business units of a company come together for a town hall meeting or an annual report. What happens? The finance people all sit together in one area. So do the IT folks, the operations team, and all other specialized units that are a part of the business. Each group has a comfort level with the people they regularly interact with. This not only deters larger scale communication, but it is a major barrier to true collaboration among work groups. Additionally, many millennials feel that businesses are too focused on making money and not focused enough on people's personal needs. Affinity groups provide them with a sense of social belonging within the business. They contribute greatly towards helping millennials to be engaged, be productive, and desire to stay with a company that provides this type of social bonding.

Creating the Plan: "What we can do about it"

First, you must put the formation of affinity groups in the hands of the employees. Leadership driven affinity groups seldom work because younger generations see that as another form of hierarchy. And as we have already seen, businesses should be seeking opportunities to minimize the hierarchies. Encourage all generations to both lead and participate. Begin by launching an interest-finding mission throughout your business. Find a champion with a solid interest in whatever that groups commonality will be and empower them to seek out others who have that common interest. As groups begin to form, encourage them to spread the word about that group's purpose. Remember that the purpose of affinity groups is to bring people together, not separate them. Think of them as inclusion groups and see that they are open to all people interested in the group regardless of whether they fit the model or not. An example would be to encourage anyone who has an interest in veteran's affairs to join that group whether they have personally served or not.

Second, it is important that everyone truly understands the meaning of the group. Even though these groups are by design a social avenue for people to communicate and contribute around a common theme, there still needs to be some structure. Individuals or small groups will need to be in charge of meeting planning, agenda topics for discussion, internal communication, and external communication. The entire business should be informed of the good things that are happening within the group. Some tools to help achieve this are charter statements, purpose statements, and/or objectives. Try to keep these simple. The objective here is to provide basic structure without making the organization heavy.

Remember that while these groups are autonomous from the business, they are still a part of the business. The time spent with affinity group meeting should not interfere with regular business activities. The business, however, has the option to sponsor special events where the affinity group can add value to the business. Be sure to keep the leadership of the business informed of what is going on within the group (external communications). It is also important to remember that the overarching purpose of these groups is to bring people of all generations together to increase harmony and productivity within the business. The affinity groups cannot become more important than the workplace objectives or they will defeat their purpose. As the group grows, it will bring people together and hopefully provide a benefit to the business.

So what else can affinity groups do? Other than creating a space for people of all generations who share common interests to come together, they are an excellent forum for identifying mentoring opportunities. They also open doors for alternative learning opportunities. And they can create opportunities to celebrate diversity within the business. When two or more groups socialize together, there is space for in-depth learning and awareness of each other's unique contributions to the organization. And they provide a way to give back to others through community service.

Why is this important? What will it mean to your business?

Affinity groups have a positive influence on the workforce of the business in many ways. Some of the ways they add value to the business are:

- People who feel connected are more loyal to the business.
- Through affinity groups, millennials can fulfill their need for social contribution.
- Affinity groups provide all generations with a sense of belonging.
- They build and strengthen relationships.
- They promote open communication.
- They act as a stress reliever.
- They allow millennials a platform to demonstrate credibility to others.
- They create work/life/community service balance within the workplace.
- They foster collaboration and creativity.
- They allow millennials and Generation Zers to compete with older generations on an even playing field.
- They promote a better understanding of other's strengths, opportunities, and interests.
- They become a recruiting and retention tool by identifying the workplace as a best place to work.

Inject Technology: Make It Fun

Understanding the Challenge: It Is the Way of the Future for All of Us

Baby boomers and Gen Xers have had the luxury of seeing technology grow over a fairly long period of time. Millennials have been immersed in it from their earliest years. Just like learning a foreign language, technology is easier to adopt when it is a part of everything around you. There is no denying that technology has put a wealth of information at our fingertips. We need to remember, however, that what we gain from the internet is knowledge and example. We don't master skills and become competent until we demonstrate the application of that knowledge. Millennials tend to make that transition faster than boomers or Gen Xers. It is important to remember two things about the millennial generation. Many of them have gained much knowledge from watching videos, particularly YouTube. They also see their devices (smartphones) primarily as a communication tool and secondarily as a business tool. As social networks continue to evolve, interpersonal reliance on handheld technology will continue to become more important. New platforms and applications that are business-oriented are emerging every day. Remember, too, that dependence on technology creates a lack of interpersonal skills that might be required for other roles or positions. There is no need to retain information that can readily be re-Googled. This can lead to people not developing good problem-solving skills and/ or analytical skills. The business world needs to embrace these changes. Smart business leaders will look for way to incorporate them into their business culture. This is even more critical as Generation Z becomes a larger part of the workforce. This generation has been connected from birth. All of their experience is with digital communication. And as a generation, they have shut down to non-technology-based tools.

Creating the Plan: "What we can do about it"

First and foremost, businesses need to be aware of emerging technology that can transform their workplace to one where younger talent feels comfortable. Many new platforms merge business needs with social connectivity. Those companies that embrace the evolution of technology will emerge as the progressive businesses of the future.

While older generations are more comfortable with face-to-face relationships, we must admit that technology brings a speed to the business that has never before been accomplished. Learning to not only embrace but master digital communication can reduce lag times in business in many ways. Encouraging millennials to mentor boomers and Gen Xers is an excellent way to bring generations together. Additionally, millennials generally have a much deeper knowledge and competence with most technologies than their older counterparts.

Like it or not, everyone is looking to online social media as a preferred way to stay connected. Preventing people from accessing platforms like Facebook, Twitter, Snapchat, and so on at work is nearly impossible. Instead of trying to minimize people's time spent perusing those applications, smart companies are finding ways to incorporate them into their culture. There are many commercial products designed for business that mimic the familiar tools. A small investment in one of those can create a pathway to transfer the time and attention lost to external communication into business information and communication that benefit the business. Instead of denying the use of those tools, reframe the action to one that has value to your business.

It is predicted that in the very near future, video will replace practically all hard copy publications. The millennial generation (and even more so the upcoming Generation Z) have learned to rely heavily on video as both a learning and entertainment tool. Businesses need to begin transforming their learning libraries into video format. Progressive companies will see having 100 percent video learning sources as a much more effective tool to grow their businesses. The ability to push training to individuals and create on-demand learning increases efficiency within the business as well. A great way to implement this is by leveraging the in-depth knowledge of the younger generations. Create opportunities for them to teach the older people how to easily create, edit, and share video on their smartphones. Many of the platforms mentioned earlier have the capacity to upload video. Encourage your people to create and share small videos that have positive impact on your business. This could be in the form of a new best practice, a success story, or even a motivational vignette that helps to bring people together.

Gaming is incredibly popular with the millennial generation. Creating a gaming environment within your business is a great way to tie skills, behaviors, and results together in a fun atmosphere. Think in terms of levels and provide opportunities to "level up" through accomplishments. Business environment game platforms are readily available on the internet. Or, maybe you have capable game developers within your business. An internal contest to develop a game concept can produce outstanding results much more cost effectively. Make the leaders in achievement visible through a leaderboard. In doing this, you will create a competitive, fun, and effective way to drive results within your business. Additionally, you will provide an opportunity for your millennial employees to interact with their smartphones in an internal business application.

Why is this important? What will it mean to your business?

Technology, and especially video, is the wave of the future. Businesses will never again resemble the workplaces of the older generations. Video is not only a progressive way to keep your business connected internally but it is a great way to stay connected with vendors and customers. Tools are readily available to allow security and privacy as you move to enhancing your company's image. Millennials and Gen Zers will have a greater comfort level using the latest and greatest offerings as well. Companies that go down this road will also have an advantage when attracting and retaining the upcoming talent. As progressive generations enter the workforce, they will be more highly dependent on their smartphones. A growing number of applicants now rely entirely on their smart devices when searching and applying for professional positions. This number will only continue to grow. Not having applications that allow job searchers to access your onboarding via their smartphone will greatly diminish the field of applicants available to you.

Internally, using progressive technology will allow the younger generations to remain more highly engaged. And as we know, engagement leads to productivity. Being quick to integrate video technology will greatly enhance your ability to manage change within your business. "Pushing" instructional video to the correct people on a predictable timeline ensures the most effective and efficient knowledge transfer. Using on-demand video will also create more effective training to policies and procedures, many of which can lead to reduced costs when it comes to human resource compliance. And, it will lead to a more harmonious and fun community across all generations.

CHAPTER 8

Keys to Success

So far, we have helped you learn about people. We have looked at how people's backgrounds and life experiences have shaped their thinking, decision-making, and behavior. We have helped you understand why people do the things they do, and we have helped you see how silly it can be when people look at the workplace purely from their own generational perspective. We have also looked at activities businesses can implement to help bring the generations together into a harmonious and productive workplace.

There are, however, other considerations we need to look at to fully unify generations in the workplace. Each generation needs to have perspective on what they can do to build bridges with other generations. In this chapter we want to clearly define specific themes associated with different generations and what people need to remember in working across generations. We will look at these from the perspective of work environment, learning and development, work ethic, work relationships, work motivation, leadership, performance feedback, and general thoughts. Fully understanding and appreciating the underlying traits of generations other than our own opens the door for effective communication and harmony.

THINGS BABY BOOMERS AND GENERATION XERS NEED TO REMEMBER WHEN WORKING WITH MILLENNIALS

Millennials are primarily the children of baby boomers and older Gen Xers. Many of their traits and characteristics are derived from the influence of their parents. Clearly, millennials, and the homes in which they were raised, are unique. People of all generations are individuals; they think, act, and make decisions based on their own experiences. There are, however, overarching themes that represent the millennial generation. Among them are:

- **Work Environment** – Millennials place high value on their friends and lifestyle. They draw more value from these than they do work compared to previous generations. They don't believe that the primary purpose of a business should be to make money. They generally feel that the senior business leaders' primary goal is to get rich. The millennial generation is very focused on community service. If you are of an older generation and you are working with a millennial, try to understand where they are coming from. Help them see that you are working from models that have proved to be successful. Look for ways to promote opportunities where they can serve the community, thereby helping them balance their lives.
- **Learning and Development** – Millennials were raised to believe that education is the key to success. They want to be continually developed professionally in the workplace, and they often equate development with success. As you work with

millennials, keep them motivated by having some form of learning implemented into their work. Follow up with them frequently as to their learning. They will appreciate your interest in their growth, and it will go a long way towards building solid relationships with them.

- **Work Ethic** – Millennials were raised to equate tasks with having fun. Their activities were scheduled by their very busy parents. There was little pressure on them to work hard. As such, they generally want to be told what to do instead of recognizing what needs to be done. The transition from an "everybody wins" world to the highly competitive business world is hard for them. Slow down and take the time to help them adapt to a workplace that is unlike what they have experienced in the past.

- **Work Relationships** – The millennial generation prefers to work in groups, but they see a high level of competition within those groups. They will be very loyal to leaders if they feel those leaders care about them, and they will leave a job quickly if they don't feel that connection. Be intentional about understanding them as individuals. Each of them will have a preferred way to communicate with you. Work with them and be open-minded as you figure out the best way to communicate with each other.

- **Work Motivation** – Millennials see work as the time between weekends and/or activities they have planned. Work is a means to their life experiences. They are highly educated and have confidence in themselves. However, their ways might not be your ways. Ask them what characteristics or actions they see as contributors to their success and work within those areas. Encourage them and praise them for not only success but progress towards goals.

- **Leadership** – Millennials generally do not like to take orders. They have a strong sense of needing to know the "why" before taking on a task or assignment. They like to figure things out for themselves (using the internet). They will quickly leave a job they don't like. They tend to be impatient, but they genuinely want to learn. And they learn quickly with the proper work direction. They want to be advised by qualified mentors. Involve them in the process by taking time to ask their opinions. They will understand if not everything goes their way, but they do want to be heard.

- **Performance Feedback** – Millennials want and need continual and timely feedback to feel confident that they are on track. They want to make an impact but will easily question the status quo. They were taught to ask for what they want, and they feel entitled to raises and promotions. Transitioning from safety and security of home to the challenges of the workplace has been hard on them, and they tend to revert back to what they have experienced in the past when they feel like life is too hard. This generation is more apt to move back in with parents than any previous generation. Help them grow and become confident by taking time to tell them when they are doing well and redirect them quickly if they appear to be moving off track.

- **General** – Millennials like to form relationships through groups. Hence, they are slower to form individual relationships. Millennials get married and have children later than previous generations and think about life "in the real world" later than previous generations. They might not be as responsive to sitting in your office and opening up to you. Although that might be a comfort zone for you, remember that they are much more used to digital communication. Help them feel comfortable by spending a little time talking about their life away from work before jumping in to business related topics. Try to keep conversations on the same level rather than as a superior talking to a subordinate.

THINGS MILLENNIALS NEED TO REMEMBER WHEN WORKING WITH BABY BOOMERS AND GEN XERS

Baby boomers and Generation Xers are also individuals who are a product of their experiences and environment. Millennials need to understand the changes that these people have experienced throughout their work history. Culture and technology have both seen numerous revolutions during their lifetime. As such, they might be more analytical of change in the workplace and be more apt to make sure it is long-term before adopting it. They like to stick with the tried and true. They have good intentions for you and the business, but they too have overarching themes that define them. Among them are:

- **Work Environment** – Older generations have spent many
  years working in traditional work places. Only recently have
  technological advances been implemented. Although they
  might be familiar with newer technologies, they might not
  be comfortable with them. They often don't see technology as
  the solution to every challenge like younger generations are
  accustomed to. Respect their commitment to the business.
  Understand that the primary purpose of any business is to
  make a profit. Positively affecting society and individual lives
  are byproducts of the business being successful. Change can be
  hard for them, so be patient with them. If you use your skills
  and talents to be focused on the business needs, they will gladly
  work with you to achieve the balance of life that you desire.
- **Learning and Development** – Boomers and Gen Xers learn
  by reading books and studying. Online learning is fairly new
  to them. Although they embrace it, it might not be the first
  direction they turn when looking for answers. Whereas you
  grew up with ever-changing technology and learned each as
  they emerged, this is all fairly new to older generations. Many

struggle with so many new platforms, and many are fearful of technology. Never tell them, "This is easy." Instead, help them overcome their fear by showing them that technology really can help them be better and more efficient at their work.

- **Work Ethic** – Older generations were taught that you are to work hard and see the task through to completion. They are very results driven and will follow established processes in order to achieve completion. They tend to put the business and their work ahead of their personal life. As you interact with them, make an effort to understand them. Let them know that you understand their drive to get results. Ask them to help you learn more about how you can contribute to that. It will go a long way to make you successful in your career.

- **Work Relationships** – Baby boomers and Gen Xers grew up in extremely hierarchically workplaces. As such, they learned to listen to those who had more experience than them. They generally saw their next advancement as the role of their current leader, meaning as their leader retired or moved on, they would move into that role. They were collaborators but also competitive. Try to understand where they have come in their careers. Tell them what the ideal work environment looks like to you. Be willing to compromise in order to create a fun but productive workplace.

- **Work Motivation** – For older generations, climbing the corporate ladder was the overall vision of advancement and success. They are very fond of business titles and will work hard to achieve those positions and titles. There is a much closer relationship between work and personal life for them. They are willing to work long hours to achieve results. As you work with them, be willing to work a few extra hours at the office in order to show them your commitment.

- **Leadership** – Boomers and Gen Xers have been taught what leadership is in a hundred ways, from a hundred different people. Their personal leadership style will be a conglomerate of all of the influences they have experienced. No two people will lead exactly the same way. They also have learned to be very loyal to their leaders and will follow direction with little questioning. Be willing to follow at times before you fully understand their motives. Know that they have your best interest at heart. Respect what they have learned through their experiences and strive to learn from them. They can help you quickly assimilate into company culture.

- **Performance Feedback** – Older generations came of age professionally in a time where feedback was given in the form of annual performance reviews. They are not accustomed to giving regular and timely feedback. Although they agree that this is preferable, it is usually not a part of their work culture. Don't be afraid to tell them how you want feedback. Ultimately, since they are results driven, they will learn to give you what you need in regard to your own feedback.

- **General** – Boomers and Gen Xers have been around the business world a long time and have experienced many things. They have learned more about the realistic and practical side of business than could ever be learned through formal training. They do care about you professionally and want to see you be successful. They don't adapt to societal changes as quickly as you do. Talk to them; ask them questions. Strive to learn more about who they are. In doing so, you will create relationships with the very people who can guide you to success in your career.

CHAPTER 9

A Real Story of Generational Dysfunction

All of the scenarios portrayed in this story are based on real situations that have been captured through an extensive interview process. The main fictional characters will be familiar to you. We came to know Walt, Nancy, Bill, and Ashlee earlier of this book. Knowing them will add context to understanding why they behave the way they do. All other characters are purely fictitious.

Sawgrass Engineering, Inc., was formed in the summer of 1951. It began as a one-man shop with its owner, Walter Robertson, doing whatever work he could muster. The post-World War II era was a good time to be involved in the building industry. The new concept of planned housing developments was springing up everywhere, and the Richmond, Virginia, area was one of the places that led the way. With the influx of people came the need for stores and services to make life convenient. Walt's little firm was soon becoming a trusted part of getting these new building projects off the ground. Before long, he had five additional engineers working in the business. The big break came in 1954 when he landed a contract to build six new A&P grocery stores around the Richmond area. This launched his success, and he never looked back.

Over the years, the business went through several expansions. As a civil engineering business, they soon had branched out into doing utility, transportation, commercial, and retail projects in addition to their work for the growing municipalities around the Richmond area. Walt was extremely proud on the September day in 1964 when they cut the ribbon on their new office space in Midlothian. He was even more proud when his daughter Nancy came on board in 1985 as the company's new director of operations. Nancy had cut her teeth running large projects for her previous employers. She also brought expertise in their industry, having spent two years on the Richmond planning commission. The team at Sawgrass was glad that she was a part of their family. Walt was proud that she was a part of his. Her work ethic and attention to detail earned the respect of everyone with whom she came in contact. She was much more than the boss's daughter.

Walt had always enjoyed vacationing in Charleston, South Carolina, and watching the women at the markets weave beautiful baskets from strands of sawgrass they picked from the water's edge. He marveled at how they could take individual blades, all looking similar, and create beautiful, colorful patterned products that were each unique. He always said that if he ever had a business of his own, he would name it Sawgrass and make sure that all of the individual people would come together to create a beautiful company just like the unique baskets. He led the business with a firm hand, being the master weaver that brought everyone together. Engineers loved working for him. They knew that his direction and guidance would keep them in the spotlight of their industry. They mirrored his dedication. The firm had a reputation for getting things done on time while building strong relationships with their clients. No one had a bad word to say about Walt and his team.

Walt was planning his retirement in 2004 when the business was rocked with the news that he suddenly died. He had been on-site with the senior leaders from Circuit City when he began to feel faint. The senior VP of development quickly dialed 911 from his cell phone, but by the time paramedics arrived it was too late. Walter Roberson left this earth doing what he loved—studying the grounds of a new store location. There were no objections when the announcement came that Nancy would be stepping up into the role of CEO.

Under her leadership, the business continued to thrive. She realized that, not being an engineer herself, she would need to bring on experienced talent to handle that aspect of the business while she focused on the C-suite operations. In June of 2011 she was introduced to a highly experienced project manager named Bill Thomas. She liked Bill from the start. He was hired to become the new COO at Sawgrass. He would have three qualified senior project managers on his team. They were each experienced engineers as well. Ben Peterson, Patrick Newburg, and Jaye McIntyre would each focus on specific types of engineering projects. Their respective teams would be able to aptly handle a multitude of projects simultaneously. She also hired three young IT specialists to keep all of their programs running and up to date. The business was running like a well-oiled machine.

Nancy modeled much of her leadership style after what she has observed from her father. She made decisions quickly and firmly but always with as much information as she could gather. She provided Bill with strong work direction and expected him to get results. She made it a point to stay out of the way of her employees and hold them accountable through Bill. Bill, in turn, relied on his direct reports to carry out the work assigned to them. They were responsible for achieving results, keeping their clients happy, and making a profit for the business. It was a well-structured hierarchy, one that would stand firm and keep the business in line.

One morning as Nancy swung her car into the parking lot, she saw something out of the ordinary. She was always the first to arrive each day, but on this day, there was already another car in the lot. She recognized the person sitting in the driver's seat as Martin Carothers, a developer with whom they had done a lot of business. She walked over to his car and greeted him. "Good morning, Martin. What brings you out here this early in the day?"

"We need to talk, Nancy. And you should know that I am not happy."

"I am sorry, Martin. Let's head into my office. I will grab us a cup of coffee."

Nancy's mind was running like a race car. She desperately tried to recall the details of the latest project they were doing together. She hated to not be mentally ready for business conversations. But she could not recall Bill informing her of anything wrong with his work. Once they made it to her office, she handed Martin his coffee, sat down behind her desk, and asked him what was on his mind.

"Nancy, you know that we have always worked well together. And I have always trusted your firm to be on time with everything you do for me. But we have a situation now that might just jeopardize our relationship."

"I am very sorry for whatever has happened, Martin. But I am not aware of anything wrong on your job. Please fill me in."

"We have a meeting with the Henrico County Planning Commission on Thursday for the new plaza we are building over in Short Pump. Last night around 6:30, I got a call from your project manager telling me that you might not be prepared to address everything in that meeting. I'm telling you, Nancy, that if we fall behind this early in the process, I just might have to find a firm that I can count on."

"I understand, Martin, and I can assure you that we will do everything necessary to be ready for that meeting. You know that you can trust us. I also know the level of importance this is to you. Can you give me a chance to get this straightened out?"

Nancy was waiting for Bill when he arrived. "We need to talk right away, Bill. Grab a cup of coffee and meet me in my office." Bill sat down and Nancy reiterated everything that Martin had told her. Bill was not aware of the situation either. Nancy directed him to find out what had happened and to do whatever was necessary to get it right. Bill knew how he was going to spend his day, and it wasn't like he had planned.

Bill knocked on Nancy's door at 1:30 that afternoon. "Got a minute?" he asked. "I can bring you up to speed on Martin's concern."

"Sure, come on in," Nancy replied.

"Well, let me start by saying that we have it under control. I pulled a couple of people over from Jaye's team to focus on picking up the slack. Here's what caused the problem in the first place. Do you remember Everette on Patrick's team? He's that thirtyish guy we hired a while back from Bernstein and Lewis. It seems that he has been less than dependable. He comes in at whatever time he feels like and has been missing entire days as well. When Patrick asked him about it, he said that he needs to handle some things at home. His wife has an executive position and because she makes more than him, he feels like it is his responsibility to do things like taking the kids to the doctor and meeting with teachers at their school. He just decided on his own that he should be able to work from home. He says that he can manage everything if we let him do that. Patrick told him that we didn't allow that here and that he needed to be in the office every day. Well, on Friday he didn't show up and didn't call in. Patrick was busy and didn't get around to checking up on him. And get this. He said that he was working from home that day and put hours on his time card. I'm having Patrick write him up. I will sit in on the disciplinary meeting as a witness in case it doesn't go well."

"Thanks Bill. I appreciate you making sure everything works out. I will call Martin and let him know that we will be totally prepared for the planning commission meeting on Thursday."

At 4:00 that afternoon, Patrick and Bill sat down to give Everette his written warning for his absence from work and for violating company policy by working from home. Everette sat quietly and listened to all Patrick had to say. When Patrick asked him if he had anything to say, Everette said, "First of all, I did call in. I sent you a text at 10:00 a.m. Secondly, I am giving you my two weeks' notice. I don't feel appreciated here, and I still don't see why I can't do my work from home. It just makes more sense to be able to do what I need to do there and still get my work done." After Everette left the office, Bill told Patrick that he would carve out some time to begin the search for a new engineer for his team. It seemed to Bill that he was always caught in the middle between Nancy's firm direction and the younger people's lack of accountability to their jobs.

A few months later, the office's administrative assistant, Shelly Rosenberg, told Nancy that she was going to retire. Shelly had been with the firm since Walt's days. Shelly told Nancy that although she still enjoyed her job, it was time to turn it over to someone younger. She gave Nancy thirty days' notice so that she would have time to train whomever Nancy hired as her replacement. Nancy reached out to her placement agency to begin finding a qualified replacement. Misti Joyner started work on the next Monday morning. Shelly met her and showed her around the office. She introduced her to everyone they saw along the way. When they got to Nancy's office, they sat down so Nancy could go over her expectations for Misti. Nancy was firm and direct. That was her style. She asked Misti if there was anything that she wanted to share with her. "Yes," Misti said. "I just want you to know that I am very sensitive, and I will cry if you yell at me." Nancy chuckled. "Misti, I don't think I have ever yelled at anyone at work. My daughter at home, maybe. But never at work." Misti went on to tell her that this was only her second job. She left the last one because she didn't take criticism well. Nancy explained that it is through constructive criticism that people learn. She talked about examples from her own career where the criticism she received made her work harder and accomplish more. Nancy used all of her baby boomer skills to let her know that they could turn her into a first-rate administrative assistant. Misti sat there expressionless. Her millennial mind wasn't fully processing much of what was being shared.

Nancy turned Misti over to Shelly and went back to her work. Once again, it seemed like the older people and the younger ones were speaking different languages. Before long, Misti was complaining to Nancy that she didn't have enough time to fulfill everyone's needs. She seemed to pick the ones she wanted to work with and let things fall through the cracks for others. Travel reservations were being done incorrectly and meeting invitations were not being sent. Nancy began to realize that she probably made a poor choice for the assistant. She observed Misti spending a lot of time talking to others. Far too many times she would see her using her phone at her desk. Nancy approached Misti about the perception of wasting time. When she mentioned the office talking, Misti told Nancy that she saw networking as a part of her job. Nancy didn't recall that being in the job description. Eventually the leaders stopped asking her to do things for them. It was easier for the baby boomers and Gen Xers to just do things themselves.

The business continued to flourish under Nancy and Bill's leadership. Their work for the municipalities in and around the Richmond area expanded to sewer and water line expansion into new developments, redesigning numerous intersections, and a major new water treatment facility. The workload flowed smoothly down the chain to those who performed the work. The success and profits flowed back up the chain to those who could reinvest it in the business. Sawgrass Engineering, Inc., was running near peak capacity. Nancy and Bill added the necessary resources to make sure all company objectives were met.

In March of 2017, Henrico County approached them once again. They were committing to a major overhaul of their fire protection capability. So many new suburbs had grown up that the capacity to provide fire protection was now inadequate. They had plans to add seven additional local fire stations. Because of the relationship Sawgrass had built with them, they wanted them to handle all of the site design. This would turn out to be one of the largest contracts in Sawgrass's history. It was imperative that it be done correctly. Bill pulled together a team of the best they had from each of the project manager's resources. Nancy scrambled to locate backfill engineers to keep the rest of the business running.

The team that Bill assembled consisted of six engineers, a senior project manager, and an intern. They all met in the conference room at 8:00 the following Monday morning to create a project plan. Roles were assigned, timelines were set, and checkpoints were established. Each of the engineers would take responsibility for one of the proposed sites. The senior project manager would take the last one and be assisted by their intern. Eric the senior manager asked Josh the intern if he felt comfortable with this role. "Well, to be perfectly honest with you, I am not real confident. Would it be possible for me to shadow one of the other engineers so that I can better understand the scope of the project?" Eric ran this by Bill, and even though Bill didn't feel like that exercise would produce a positive outcome, he agreed. Josh would shadow Tracey on Wednesday.

On Wednesday afternoon, Bill stopped by Josh's desk to see what he had learned in the shadowing. "Well, I didn't exactly do that," Josh told him.

"Why not?" Bill asked. "What did you do today instead?"

"Tracey was out today. Since I was supposed to be with him, and he wasn't here, I didn't know what to do. I just stayed here at my desk and read things online."

Bill was livid with Josh, not only for wasting a day's work but for not asking for direction when the situation changed. Still, he bit his tongue and made a point to talk to Eric about it. An hour later, Josh stopped by Bill's office to ask if, since he hadn't been able to shadow that day, he could shadow with someone else the next day. Bill was speechless. *Every time I have to deal with millennials, they wear me out*, he thought to himself.

At the team meeting the following Monday, they realized that there was a technical problem that would need to be resolved. Not all of the people on the team were using the latest release of AutoCAD on their computers. It would be critical to the success of the project for them all to be using AutoCAD 2018 in order to access all of the files in the libraries. Bill filed a ticket with IT to get all of the computers upgraded. The team went on with their work but was noticeably slowed because of the inability to share files.

One of the standing agenda items for their weekly meetings was to follow up on the progress of the ticket. After two weeks of "in progress" status notifications, Bill decided to contact IT directly. "Who is the lead on the IT team?" he asked Eric.

"It's that girl we hired about six months ago. I think her name is Ashlee Williams," Eric told him. "She came to us from a very successful firm in Colorado."

Bill dialed Ashlee's number. Her phone rang five times and then went to voicemail. He hung up and dialed again. Once more it went to voicemail. "Josh, will you please go down there and ask Ashlee to come up to this meeting? I need an answer on this." Josh left and returned ten minutes later by himself.

"Wasn't she there?" Bill asked Josh.

"Oh yeah, she was there," Josh told him.

"Then why isn't she here?" Bill inquired.

"Well, she said that she wasn't really comfortable coming into this meeting. It's something about a previous job she had in Texas. She said that she does much better on Skype, but she will pick up the phone if you call her."

Bill felt his blood pressure rise as he dialed Ashlee's number once again. He was mentally creating scenarios on how to deal with her. Ashlee picked up the call on the fifth ring. Bill put her on the speaker so everyone could contribute to the conversation. "Good morning, Ashlee. You are the lead on the IT team, correct?"

"Yeah, I am. What do you need from me today?"

"Ashlee, I am here with the strategic team working on the Henrico fire station project. We have you on speakerphone so everyone can hear our conversation. A couple of weeks ago we submitted a ticket to get everyone's computers upgraded to AutoCAD 2018. It is critical to this project that we are all using the same version so we can file share. I understand that there hasn't been any action taken on this ticket yet. Can you please help me understand why that is?"

"Let me look at the ticket. Give me just a minute." The phone was silent from Ashlee's side for several minutes. The project team patiently waited. When Ashlee came back, she said, "I see that it was supposed to go to procurement to purchase the licenses. That's out of my control. Not my fault. I'm not responsible for anything over there."

"But, Ashlee," Bill said, "don't you own the tickets?"

"Well, yeah, but we only do so much over here."

"Knowing how critical this is to the business, don't you think you might have made a note to follow up and make sure it stayed on track?"

"I still don't feel like this is my fault. It's just how the process works."

"I am very familiar with the process, Ashlee. I wrote it." Bill was growing more and more impatient with Ashlee's excuses. "I am charging you right now to make this your priority and make sure that this is completed as quickly as possible. Do you understand me, Ashlee?"

"I don't know why you need to yell at me. I will see what I can do."

As soon as Bill hung up the phone, he called accounting and asked what they knew about the purchase of the licenses. After a quick check of the records, they reported that the purchase had been completed nearly two weeks prior and the required licenses were with IT awaiting the install.

The software was updated within twenty-four hours. The team's contingency plan allowed them to get back on schedule quickly. The project moved forward as planned. Bill knew that he needed to bring Nancy up to speed. He walked down to her office and knocked on her door.

"Nancy, there is something you need to know."

"What's up, Bill?"

"Our IT team missed getting the AutoCAD 2018 upgrade in. They are doing it right now, but it is going to take a while."

"OK, I guess that is just one of those things. Any impact to the business?"

"As a matter of fact, there is. That's what I need to tell you. We are in danger of missing a deadline of document preparation for Henrico

County. There's a chance we won't be ready for the planning commission meeting. The client is really pissed."

"How did this happen, Bill?"

"As near as I can figure, the ticket to do the upgrade never got worked. It was assigned to the new girl, Ashlee. It seems that she has already become somewhat of a ringleader in the IT group. When I talked to her about it, she acted like she really didn't care. In fact, neither did any of those other millennial IT geniuses we hired."

"Let's just fire all of them and replace them with people our age, people we know will get the job done without being a pain in the ass."

"You know we can't do that, Nance. These kids have a lot of knowledge about technology that we are still trying to understand."

Nancy sat contemplatively and stared down at her notebook. Slowly, she got out of her chair and walked over to the picture of Walt above the head of the conference table. "Things were so much easier when you were here, Dad," she said to his image. "Employees then were really employees. These kids just don't get it. It wears me out to have to deal with them. I want you to be proud of me, but I'm not sure what to do."

Bill knew what he needed to do. The meeting with himself, Ashlee, and Nancy was set for Friday afternoon.

The three of them met in the conference room at 3:00. Bill began the conversation by introducing Ashlee to Nancy. He made certain that each of them understood the role, title, and their responsibilities to the business. He summarized the situation for Nancy. Then he asked Ashlee to explain what had happened from her perspective. Ashlee put up her defensive shields. She was noticeably uncomfortable. In her head, words were forming that she would not let out. Her need for belonging in her workplace was overshadowed by her unwillingness to take responsibility. However, taking responsibility was what Bill and Nancy were all about. Although Ashlee was well aware that her failure to stay on top of the ticket caused the problem, she continually made excuses, putting the blame on others. Ashlee told Bill and Nancy that she saw herself as "self-advocating." In the end, the meeting closed without any of them feeling like anything was accomplished.

Ashlee returned to her work area thinking about moving back in with her mom in Colorado. Bill walked away, contemplating the balance between his work and personal life. He struggled with the desire to do whatever it took to make his work successful but was wondering what the toll was on his wife, Jessica, and the dreams they had of spending more time together. Was dealing with these millennial kids even worth it? Maybe there was a better way to work with them. Maybe they should just give in and not hold these kids accountable, but, then again, how would the business survive if he did that? *They just don't care about anything but themselves*, he thought to himself. Nancy returned to the picture of her father above the conference table. "I do my best, Dad. I try to use everything you taught me. Things just aren't the same anymore. It seems like we just can't depend on these younger people. We need them in our work. They are the future, and they have so much knowledge. I just can't figure out how to make them realize that we have commitments to customers, let alone that we need to make a profit. Things were so much easier when people wanted to work hard. Sawgrass Engineering has been our life, but I am having trouble bringing the human fronds together to make something beautiful. Maybe it's time for me to step aside and get someone in here who knows how to work with them. Life at a beach house is looking pretty good right now. Thank you, Dad, for all you taught me. I love you."

CHAPTER 9

A Real Story of Generational Dysfunction (Do-over)

Sawgrass Engineering, Inc., was formed in the summer of 1951. It began as a one-man shop with its owner, Walter Robertson, doing whatever work he could muster. The post-World War II era was a good time to be involved in the building industry. The new concept of planned housing developments was springing up everywhere, and the Richmond, Virginia, area was one of the places that led the way. With the influx of people came the need for stores and services to make life convenient. Walt's little firm was soon becoming a trusted part of getting these new building projects off the ground. Before long, he had five additional engineers working in the business. The big break came in 1954 when he landed a contract to build six new A&P grocery stores around the Richmond area. He was successful, and he would never look back.

Over the years, the business went through several expansions. As a civil engineering business, they soon had branched out into doing utility, transportation, commercial, and retail projects in addition to their work for the growing municipalities around the Richmond area. Walt was extremely proud on the September day in 1964 when they cut the ribbon on their new multilevel office space in Midlothian. He was even more proud when his daughter Nancy came on board in 1985 as the company's new director of operations. Nancy had cut her teeth running large projects for her previous employers. She also brought expertise in their industry, having spent two years on the Richmond planning commission. The team at Sawgrass was glad that she was a part of their family. Walt was proud that she was a part of his. Her work ethic and attention to detail earned the respect of everyone with whom she came in contact. She was much more than the boss's daughter.

Walt had always enjoyed vacationing in Charleston, South Carolina, and watching the women at the markets weave beautiful baskets from strands of sawgrass they picked from the water's edge. He marveled at how they could take individual blades, all looking similar, and create beautiful, colorful patterned products that were each unique. He always said that if he ever had a business of his own, he would name it Sawgrass and make sure that all of the individual people would come together to create a beautiful company just like the unique baskets. He led the business with a firm hand, being the master weaver that brought everyone together. Engineers loved working for him. They knew that his direction and guidance would keep them in the spotlight of their industry. They mirrored his dedication. The firm had a reputation for getting things done on time while building strong relationships with their clients. No one had a bad word to say about Walt and his team.

Walt was planning his retirement in 2004 when the business was rocked with the news that he suddenly died. He had been on-site with the senior leaders from Circuit City when he began to feel faint. The senior VP of development quickly dialed 911 from his cell phone, but by the time paramedics arrived it was too late. Walter Roberson left this earth doing what he loved—studying the grounds of a new store location. There were no objections when the announcement came that Nancy would be stepping up into the role of CEO.

Under her leadership, the business continued to thrive. She realized that, not being an engineer herself, she would need to bring on experienced talent to handle that aspect of the business while she focused on the C-suite operations. Nancy had also learned that she needed people more than people needed her. She had been fortunate to work under a leader at Dominion Energy that understood the value in creating a workplace where everyone could do their best. She had learned that everyone regardless of title, seniority, or experience had something to learn. She knew that she would need to create a culture at Sawgrass that would work for everyone. She made it a point to be open-minded and learn everything she could about people at every opportunity. In June of 2011 she was introduced to a highly experienced project manager named Bill Thomas. She liked Bill from the start. He was hired to become the new COO at Sawgrass. He would have three qualified senior project managers on his team. They were each experienced engineers as well. Ben Peterson, Patrick Newburg, and Jaye McIntyre would each focus on specific types of engineering projects. Their respective teams would be able to aptly handle a multitude of projects simultaneously. She also hired three young IT specialists to keep all of their programs running and up to date. The business was running like a well-oiled machine. One of her first steps in creating a positive culture was to form an advisory team made up of representatives from all departments and ages. This team was brought together with the mission of discovering what the people of the business wanted from leadership from a personal perspective.

They learned several things:

- Leadership was perceived as being strict and inflexible. Work direction was commanded instead of shared.
- A lot of the younger people felt unappreciated. They felt like their knowledge wasn't being utilized by the business.

- Everyone seemed to be ultra-focused on their own contribution to the process. They were very compartmentalized. There was little to no communication across business functions unless there was an emergency.

Nancy knew that if they could tackle these areas, they could bring unity to their offices. She also knew that when that happened, engagement and productivity would go up. Not only was this the best thing to do for the business but it was the right thing to do for the people.

Nancy modeled much of her leadership style after what she has observed from her father. She made decisions quickly and firmly but always with as much information as she could gather. But she also adapted her style to be receptive to change when it would benefit the business. She worked together with Bill to gain his full commitment to his mission and direction. However, she still expected him to get the results that matched the company's business plan. She made it a point to listen to her employees and be open to what they had to say. Everyone was still held accountable for their contributions to success. Bill, in turn, learned to work through his direct reports in the same manner. They were responsible for their team's quality and deadlines, keeping their clients and direct reports happy, and making a profit for the business. A structure of bi-weekly one-on-one meetings was established throughout the business. These meetings were time that leaders set aside to listen to those who worked with them. They also focused on each person's individual development within the company. It was a well-structured community, one that would be collaborative and keep the business productive. Nancy also learned that the traditional layers of management in her business suppressed communication and trust. She began to look for ways to take some of the layers out without compromising the business's success. She realized that she didn't need to remove job titles, but she needed to teach her leaders how to remove the perception of hierarchy. She found a talent development consultant that could help her with that.

The benefit of their advanced knowledge of working with people far outweighed the minimal cost to the business. Their plan was easy to implement and yielded results almost immediately.

One morning as Nancy swung her car into the parking lot, she saw something out of the ordinary. She was always the first to arrive each day, but on this day, there was already another car in the lot. She recognized the person sitting in the driver's seat as Martin Carothers, a developer with whom they had done a lot of business. She walked over to his car and greeted him. "Good morning, Martin. What brings you out here this early in the day?"

"We need to talk, Nancy. And you should know that I am not happy."

"I am sorry, Martin. Let's head into my office. I will grab us some coffee."

Nancy's mind was running like a race car. She desperately tried to recall the details of the latest project they were doing together. She hated to not be mentally ready for business conversations. But she could not recall Bill informing her of anything wrong with his project. Once they made it to her office, she handed Martin his coffee, sat down behind her desk, and asked him what was on his mind.

"Nancy, you know that we have always worked well together. And I have always trusted your firm to be on time with everything you do for me. But we have a situation now that might just jeopardize our relationship."

"I am very sorry for whatever has happened, Martin. But I am not aware of anything wrong on your job. Please fill me in."

"We have a meeting with the Henrico County Planning Commission on Thursday for the new plaza we are building over in Short Pump. Last night around 6:30, I got a call from your project manager telling me that you might not be prepared to address everything in that meeting. I'm telling you, Nancy, that if we fall behind this early in the process, I just might have to find a firm that I can count on."

"I understand, Martin, and I can assure you that this is not how we work here. I will do everything necessary to see that we are ready for that meeting. You know that you can trust us. I also know the level of importance this is to you. Can you give me a chance to get this straightened out?"

Nancy was waiting for Bill when he arrived. "We need to talk right away, Bill. Grab a cup of coffee and meet me in my office." Bill sat down and Nancy reiterated everything that Martin had told her. Bill was not aware of the situation either. Nancy directed him to find out what had happened and come back to her so that they could devise a plan together to correct the situation. Bill realized that this was going to take some time from his day, but he was already formulating a plan to work through it. He knew Nancy would support him.

Bill knocked on Nancy's door at 1:30 that afternoon. "Got a minute?" he asked. "I can bring you up to speed on Martin's concern."

"Sure, come on in," Nancy replied.

"Well, let me start by saying that we have it under control. I pulled a couple of people over from Jaye's team to focus on picking up the slack. Here's what caused the problem in the first place. Do you remember Everette on Patrick's team? He's that thirtyish guy we hired a while back from Bernstein and Lewis. It seems that he has been less than dependable. He comes in at whatever time he feels like and has been missing entire days as well. Patrick has been talking with him about it. His basic challenge stems from some problems he is having at home. His wife has an executive position and because she makes more than him, he feels like doing things like taking the kids to the doctor and meeting with teachers at their school is his responsibility. He has asked that he be allowed to work from home a couple of days a week. He says that he can manage everything if we let him do that. Patrick told him that even though we had never done that before, it might be a possibility. He told Everette to give him a day or two to bring it up with me."

"Well, on Friday, before we had a chance to talk, Everette couldn't make it in. He sent Patrick a text message, but evidently Patrick didn't see it until late in the day. I reminded Patrick of the importance of agreeing with each of his people on the way they want to communicate. He told me that Everette had let him know that texting was his preferred method to communicate. Patrick just missed it. It was an honest mistake; he understands now. It won't happen again. We can put that to rest. "What do you think, Nancy? Can we let Everette try the working from home thing? We can set some good guardrails around how that needs to look and what our expectations will be. He's a good guy and brings a lot of value to Sawgrass. I think this will keep him with us if we can make it work. Who knows? Maybe it can be a model for others to be able to do the same thing. I will have Patrick create a plan around trying this out with Everette. Let's give it a thirty-day trial. I will put a follow-up meeting on our calendars to get together and look at the results."

"Thanks, Bill. I appreciate you making sure everything works out. I have never thought of allowing people to work from home, but I certainly am not opposed to it if we can keep the business on track. This is important enough that I think we should all be involved. Let's spend an hour or two with you, me, Patrick, and Everette to create the model. I will call Martin and let him know that we will be totally prepared for the planning commission meeting on Thursday."

At 4:00 that afternoon, Patrick sat down with Everette to review what had happened. It was important to make sure that there was a full understanding of the impact it could have had to the business. He also wanted to reassure Everette that he didn't need to have any extra anxiety over the situation. He also reminded Everette that he had told him that he himself preferred face-to-face or a phone call as his primary method of communication. Everette sat quietly and listened to all Patrick had to say and apologized for not calling Patrick about his absence. Patrick also told Everette about the upcoming meeting to create a plan for him to work from home. Everette was overjoyed that the business cared enough about him to take those steps. "I really love working at Sawgrass," he told Patrick. "Not only do I feel valued, but you all really care about me. I plan on being a part of this company for a long, long time."

"I'm glad you feel that way Everette. It is important to all of us that people are highly motivated. You know that our clients appreciate that as well. You are an important part of this business and we want to work with you every way we can. I do need you to realize how important this will be to others who might be in a similar position as you. We have an opportunity here to mark Sawgrass as one of the most progressive employers in the Richmond area. We have got to do this right."

A few months later, the office's administrative assistant, Shelly Rosenberg, told Nancy that she was going to retire. Shelly had been with the firm since Walt's days. Shelly told Nancy that although she still enjoyed her job, it was time to turn it over to someone younger. She gave Nancy thirty days' notice so that she would have time to train whomever Nancy hired as her replacement. Nancy reached out to her placement agency to begin finding a qualified replacement. Misti Joyner started work the next Monday morning. Shelly met her and showed her around the office. She introduced her to everyone they saw along the way. When they got to Nancy's office, they sat down so Nancy could go over her personal expectations for Misti. Nancy was friendly and listened to Misti. That was her style. She asked Misti if there was anything that she wanted to share with her. "Yes," Misti said. "I just want you to know that I am very sensitive and I will cry if you yell at me." Nancy chuckled. "Misti, I don't think I have ever yelled at anyone. My daughter at home, maybe. But never at work. I think you will appreciate that the old style of 'master and servant' is not a part of our culture here at Sawgrass."

Misti went on to tell her that this was only her second job. She left the last one because she didn't take criticism well. Nancy explained that it is through constructive criticism that people learn. She talked about examples from her own career where the criticism she received made her work harder and accomplish more. Nancy told her about their communication programs and how they would help her create an individual development plan that would build on the strengths she already demonstrated, and to master the areas where she needed to become more competent. Learning how to use constructive criticism as a tool for betterment could be easy and non-threatening. Nancy used all of her leadership skills to let Misti know that they would help her grow into a first-rate administrative assistant. Misti sat there expressionless. Her millennial mind had never been exposed to a business leader talking like this. Nancy asked Shelly to set up one-on-one sessions with her personally until Misti felt comfortable. She knew that although she was terribly busy, the time spent with Misti would have a huge return on her investment.

Nancy turned Misti back over to Shelly and returned to her work. She had seen Misti's initial perception from others in the millennial generation and had learned that striving to understand them was the beginning of creating harmony with them. Not long after Shelly left, Misti came to Nancy saying that she felt overwhelmed. She said that she didn't have enough time to fulfill everyone's needs. She saw herself picking the people she wanted to work with and letting things fall through the cracks for others. She knew that wasn't right. She had made some mistakes with travel reservations and a few meeting invitations had not been sent. Nancy began to realize that she would need some help getting organized. Nancy had observed Misti spending a lot of time talking to others. Many times she would see her using her phone at her desk. She saw the opportunity to add "handling multiple priorities" and "time management" to Misti's individual development plan. Nancy approached Misti about her observations. When she mentioned the office talking, Misti told Nancy that she saw networking as a part of her job. Nancy didn't recall that being in the job description. Nancy told her that she had some good ideas of things Misti could do while on the job to help her get the correct focus. Misti appreciated the opportunity to learn more. Like most millennials, she felt that as long as she was learning, she was growing. The way that Sawgrass Engineering cared for her certainly made her feel more confident. Eventually she was able to handle everything the leaders asked of her. It made things better for everyone. The baby boomers and Gen Xers grew to trust her.

At Nancy and Bill's next one-on-one session, they spent some time talking about the developmental condition of the firm. They were both acutely attuned to the strategic vision for the next five years. What they weren't confident about was having enough internal bench strength in their staff to make that plan a reality. "So, Bill," Nancy asked, "we have been discussing our business continuity plan. What we will do if we should lose one of our key project managers. Where are we on that plan?"

"I feel pretty confident that Jaye, Patrick, and Ben are going to be with us for the long haul. Ben really isn't interested in moving beyond his current role. The other two are anxious to move up. That excitement might also work against us if a position would open at another firm. Our best defense against that is to keep them on a development track to prepare them for my position. Kinda' like, 'let the best man win.' It's just like the way you have been working with me to prepare me for the day that you decide to retire. Jaye is actually a little further ahead in his development, but they are both making progress. One project manager, Eric Waddell, is well into his development and should soon have the capability to move to a senior role. All of their leaders are working with them to find internal development opportunities. I learned a lot from the talent development consultant that we hired, but one of the most valuable things was doing the skip-level meetings. I always thought that my direct reports should be the ones to talk to everyone below them. But, when I started meeting with their teams without them present, I got so much more information. Not to say that they weren't doing a good job. It's just that as senior leaders, we can learn a whole lot about our business from talking to people with whom we don't usually communicate. They really appreciated me taking the time to listen to them. You were right; it really does remove some of those layers we used to have here at Sawgrass. Here's what I learned from those talks. Below our managers, we have three interns who are making great progress toward becoming project managers. I have their managers doing regular development sessions with them and I will continue to do skip-level meetings with all of them once a quarter to see where they are on their progress. I really think we are in good shape for the future. I will make a point to continue following up with you in our bi-weekly talks."

"That is a great report, Bill. I am really proud of you for mastering the skills we have worked on for you to be that well-organized. I can see that you have also become competent in strategic vision, another one of our objectives. Remember when we first started talking about that on your development plan? You are really making great progress towards becoming a CEO."

Bill felt a strong sense of pride in his accomplishment. He knew that the nontraditional learning lessons Nancy had taught him inside the business had value beyond anything he could have learned in a classroom. "I'm glad you feel that way, Nancy. It makes me feel good to know that you have confidence in me. There's one more thing I would like to run by you. Back in my college days, I met a guy at a concert in Miami. He was from Trinidad and was studying at the University of Miami. He is an interesting guy. His name is Christian Lara. We became friends and have loosely stayed in touch over the years. His son is planning on going into civil engineering but isn't sure it is right for him. Christian was wondering if it might be possible for him to come up here and spend a few days seeing what we do. His son has saved up quite a bit of money and will pay his own way. I can promise you that it won't interfere with any of our projects. Who knows, he might be someone we can groom for the future. Is it OK with you?"

"I don't see why not Bill. It might be fun to get a younger person's viewpoint on what we are doing."

"Thanks, Nance. It will probably be over his spring break. Isn't it funny how kids who live near the beach want to go up north for break? All we ever wanted to do was go south."

"I wanted the beach too. I guess 'times they are a-changing.'"

The business continued to flourish under Nancy and Bill's leadership. Their work for the municipalities in and around the Richmond area expanded to sewer and water line expansion into new developments, redesigning numerous intersections, and a major new water treatment facility. The workload flowed smoothly down the chain to those who performed the work. The success and profits flowed back up the chain to those who could reinvest it in the business. Sawgrass Engineering, Inc., was running near peak capacity. Nancy and Bill added the necessary resources to make sure all company objectives were met.

As the business grew, they realized that they needed to inject new avenues for their team to interact. It seemed to Nancy and Bill that the different teams were beginning to become compartmentalized. They knew that if they continued to go down this road, they would begin to lose interaction, communication, and innovation. Nancy challenged Bill with finding a way to bring people closer together. After some research, Bill came back to Nancy with an idea. "You know, Nance, we have formed a team of immense talent here at Sawgrass. All of that talent brings a lot of different personalities. And all those personalities create a diversity of interests. What if we could bring people who share those interests together, kind of on the side? If we find the right medium, we can bring people from all ages and departments into social groups. We can probably even find a way to create some company-sponsored community service through it as well. That would be great for our public exposure."

"Sounds like a pretty good idea, Bill. Can you give me an example?"

"Well, we have a lot of veterans. What if we created a group for those vets? It wouldn't matter whether they served in Vietnam, the Iraq wars, Afghanistan, or just the war on terror. They could talk about their experiences, concerns, and successes. I know some of our people have got to have hidden PTSD challenges. Maybe talking to others would help them. The group could do things like help to place flags on graves in the veteran's cemetery on special days as well. I think it would be great to bring veterans of all ages together. We wouldn't have to limit it to true vets either. There are lots of people who have sympathy to what veterans have done for all of us. There are also people who might have lost a loved one in war. The group could be open to anyone who feels that they would like to participate. The possibilities are wide open."

"I like that idea. I especially like the cross-generational aspect of it. It could be an awesome way to bring generations together. What do we need to do to get it started?"

"I will talk to some people to see if they have interest in helping launch it. I will try to get a representative from each generation to form the core team. I will help them write a charter so the purpose is well-defined. I also agree that having all generations on the formation team will be great for everyone. Let's start with this one. I have some thoughts about other groups we can form after we get this one up on its feet."

"Great work, Bill. You are thinking more like a CEO all the time. Let me know when you have a plan. I will pull some of our discretionary budget money in to help get the ball rolling. Set up a regular cadence of follow-up with me on this. I want to be informed of progress as we go through it."

"Having a program like this sponsored by Sawgrass will help us not only retain our talent but attract new talent as well. I am confident that it will be a strong contribution to our future success. I will create a follow-up schedule as soon as I get back to my computer."

A couple of weeks later, Bill came into Nancy's office to report on the progress. "It's going great, Nance. Actually, much better than I had hoped for. It's really cool to see the younger people sharing their service time stories with the Vietnam vets. They are really starting to come up with some great ideas on how to get more engaged in things. One of the younger people had a great idea. She said that they should create videos on their cell phones and uploads them to our intranet site. It would be a great way to share what is going on there, and it would make our site more fun. I checked with Ashlee over in IT, and she said that she could easily add a program to our site to allow video to be shared. And another thing, when some of the older guys said that they weren't comfortable shooting and uploading video, a couple of the younger people offered to help them learn how to do it. I love seeing that kind of collaboration. Imagine millennials mentoring baby boomers? Who would have ever thought that would happen? I think it's great. It might even open doors for all kinds of cross-mentoring. We need to figure out how to share this with the rest of the business. Just think . . . we can create informational videos, training videos, even 'state of the business' videos. It will be quick, easy, effective, and fun communication."

"I love it! Great work, Bill! Let's turn it over to the group to run now. Oh, by the way, tell them that I am allocating $5,000 to them to help them get more involved in community service."

In March of 2017, Henrico County approached them once again. They were committing to a major overhaul of their fire protection capability. So many new suburbs had grown up that the capacity to provide fire protection was now inadequate. They had plans to add seven additional local fire stations. Because of the relationship Sawgrass had built with them, they wanted the firm to handle all of the site design. This would turn out to be one of the largest contracts in Sawgrass's history. It was imperative that it be done correctly. Bill pulled together a team of the best they had from each of the project manager's resources. Nancy scrambled to locate backfill engineers to keep the rest of the business running.

The team that Bill assembled consisted of six engineers, a senior project manager, and an intern. They all met in the conference room at 8:00 the following Monday morning to create a project plan. Roles were assigned, timelines were set, and checkpoints were established. Each of the engineers would take responsibility for one of the proposed sites. The senior project manager would take the last one on and be assisted by their intern. Eric the senior manager asked Josh the intern if he felt comfortable with this role. "Well, to be perfectly honest with you, I am not real confident. Would it be possible for me to shadow one of the other engineers so that I can better understand the scope of the project?" Eric ran this by Bill, and Bill agreed they could try it. Josh would shadow Tracey on Wednesday.

On Wednesday afternoon, Bill stopped by Josh's desk to see what he had learned in the shadowing. "Well, I didn't exactly do that," Josh told him.

"Why not?" Bill asked. "What did you do today instead?"

"Tracey was out today. Since I was supposed to be with him, and he wasn't here, I didn't know what to do. I just stayed here at my desk and read things online."

Bill was upset with Josh, but he understood that Josh was young and didn't have the depth of experience that others had. Still, he bit his tongue and turned it into a learning lesson. He explained to Josh the importance of everyone being in a productive place every hour of the day. He connected the dots for him about how productive time impacts the business and the profitability.

Josh told Bill that he had never looked at it that way and thanked him for his guidance. "It is hard for us younger people to fully understand the culture of the business world. We weren't brought up be very accountable. I think this will be valuable to me in my career. Since I wasn't able to shadow today, would it be OK if I did that tomorrow?"

Bill told him to run it by Eric, but that as long as Eric was fine with it, he was too. *It's great to see a millennial being open to learning our culture and really wanting to make a strong contribution. Maybe working with these kids isn't as hard as I believed,* he thought to himself.

At the team meeting the following Monday, they realized that there was a technical problem that would need to be resolved. Not all of the people on the team were using the latest release of AutoCAD on their computers. It would be critical to the success of the project for them all to be using AutoCAD 2018 in order to access all of the files in the libraries. Bill filed a ticket with IT to get all of the computers upgraded. The team went on with their work but was noticeably slowed because of the inability to share files.

One of the standing agenda items for their weekly meetings was to follow up on the progress of outstanding tickets. The AutoCAD 2018 ticket was the first one they discussed. The ticket showed an "in progress" status notification. Bill decided to contact IT directly to see what was going on. "Who is the lead on the IT team?" he asked Eric.

"It's that girl we hired about six months ago. I think her name is Ashlee Williams," Eric told him.

"I know her. Let me give her a call and see what is happening with the ticket," Bill told them.

"Good luck with that," Ben said. "That girl never answers her phone."

Bill dialed Ashlee's number, let it ring twice, and then hung up. He them redialed her number. "Hi, Bill, this is Ashlee," she greeted him.

"Hi, Ashlee, can you do me a favor? I need to follow up on the ticket for the AutoCAD 2018 upgrade. It seems that there is some delay on it, and it is causing our project team valuable time. Can you please help?"

"Let me look at the ticket. Give me just a minute." The phone was silent for several minutes. The project team patiently waited. When Ashlee came back, she said, "I see that it went to procurement to purchase the licenses. That's out of my control, but I can certainly follow up with them. There are still some young accountants over there that don't quite get the big picture. They haven't had the privilege of learning from you how things like this can affect business. I assure you that this will have my full attention until I can get it straightened out. I'll let you know what I find out as soon as possible."

As soon as Bill hung up the phone, he called accounting and told them to make sure Ashlee got whatever she needed to make this happen. Even though he could have forced the issue himself, he also knew that this would be a great learning lesson for Ashlee and give her confidence in her ownership and accountability.

"OK, Bill," Eric asked after he hung up with Ashlee, "how did you do that? She has been one of the toughest millennials to work with ever since she got here."

Bill told Eric and the others about his cross-mentoring with Ashlee. "We have been working together for the last two months. She has taught me so much about how to work better in the digital world. I am even more organized since she showed me new ways to keep my files and projects stored in our cloud space. That stuff used to intimidate me, and I shied away from using it. Now, I don't know how I lived without it."

"But," Eric said, "You are the one with all of the experience. Shouldn't you be the one mentoring her?"

"That happens too, Eric. It's important that we all see ourselves as learners as well as teachers. Everyone in this company has things to share and places to grow. You saw how she took accountability and self-created a plan to follow through. She never would have had the insight to do that if I hadn't been helping her see the bigger picture of how we all need to work together. I am actually pretty proud of her for stepping up like she did."

Ashlee discovered that the procurement had been completed nearly two weeks prior, but IT had not been notified. She started thinking about how she might be able to influence some of her peers over in finance around the lessons she had learned from Bill.

The software was updated within twenty-four hours. The team's contingency plan allowed them to get back on schedule quickly. The project moved forward as planned. Bill knew that he needed to bring Nancy up to speed. He walked down to her office and knocked on her door.

"Hi, Nancy. Got a minute? There is something you need to know."

"What's up, Bill?"

"Our support team missed getting the AutoCAD 2018 upgrade in. They are doing it right now, but it is going to take a while."

"OK, I guess that is just one of those things. Any impact to the business?"

"As a matter of fact, there is. That's what I need to tell you. We have a slight danger of missing a deadline of document preparation for Henrico County. We have a plan in place, but there's a chance we won't be ready for the planning commission meeting. The client is really pissed."

"How did this happen, Bill?"

"The ticket to do the upgrade got hung up in finance and wasn't able to be worked by IT. It was assigned to the new girl Ashlee. You remember her? She's the one that has been cross-mentoring with me. It seems that she has already become somewhat of a leader in the IT group. When I talked to her about it, she took full accountability. Much different from most of the other millennial IT people we hired."

"Sometimes I feel like firing all of them and replacing them with people our age, people we know will get the job done without being a pain in the ass," Nancy came back.

"You know we can't do that, Nance. These kids have a lot of knowledge about technology that us boomers and Gen Xers are still trying to understand."

Nancy sat contemplatively and stared down at her notebook. Slowly, she got out of her chair and walked over to the picture of Walt above the head of the conference table. "Things were still so much easier when you were here, Dad," she said to his image. "Employees then were really employees. It's so hard to help these kids understand what we need to do to keep the business strong. I am trying to learn how to make everything work in harmony. We are getting there. I want you to be proud of me, but I'm not sure what to do."

Bill knew what he needed to do. The meeting with himself, Ashlee, and Nancy was set for Friday afternoon.

The three of them met in the conference room at 3:00. Bill began the conversation by introducing Ashlee to Nancy. He made sure that the conversation was easy for Ashlee. He knew from their talks that she had some hard feelings left over from her childhood when talking to people she looked up to. She still had distrust for authority, but she was working on it. It wasn't easy for her, but his support helped make her capable of being successful. He summarized the situation for Nancy. Then he asked Ashlee to explain what had happened from her perspective. Ashlee started to feel her defensive shields go up. She was noticeably uncomfortable. In her head, words were forming that she fought to suppress. Her need for belonging in the workplace reinforced her willingness to take responsibility. Ashlee knew that being accountable was what Bill and Nancy were all about. Although she was well aware that her failure to stay on top of the ticket contributed to the problem, she didn't make excuses and she didn't put the blame on others. Ashlee told Bill and Nancy that she saw herself as "self-advocating." Bill told her that he was proud of her for becoming self-advocating in a positive way. In the end, the meeting closed with Bill feeling proud of Ashlee. Nancy was elated to see that the inter-generational programs they had put in place were really making a difference. Ashlee was beaming at her new promotion to manager of IT for Sawgrass Engineering, Inc.

Ashlee returned to her work area thinking about her mom in Colorado. She couldn't wait to tell her about her promotion. She knew her mom would be proud of her. Bill continued to contemplate the balance of his life at work and at home. He still struggled with the desire to do whatever it took to make his work successful but was wondering what the toll was on his wife, Jessica, and the dreams they had of spending more time together. *Dealing with these millennial kids is a lot of work, but it really is worth it,* he thought. *Maybe there is an even a better way to work with them. So many of them struggle with the relationship between them and work. I need to get Ashlee's help to learn how others in her generation can get to the place where she is. If we can figure that out, I am sure that my career will be more balanced.*

Nancy returned to the picture of her father above the conference table. "I do my best, Dad. I try to use everything you taught me. You showed me the difference between right and wrong. More importantly, you taught me to act when I knew what was right and what was wrong. Things just aren't the same anymore. These younger generations don't do things the way we have always done them in the past. We need them in our work. They are our future, and they have so much knowledge. I have had to make some changes to our business culture. Some of them were hard for me to accept, but when I listen to people and create ways for them to talk to each other, those challenges aren't so bad. Things are so much easier when people want to work hard. Baby boomers, Gen Xers, and millennials really can understand each other when we realize that everyone is a teacher and everyone is a learner. Sawgrass Engineering has been our life. Bringing the human fronds together to make something beautiful really has made this a place of harmony where everyone can do their best. Maybe it's time for me to step aside. Bill knows how to work with them; he can lead this business to continued prosperity. Life at a beach house is looking pretty good right now. Thank you, Dad, for all you taught me. I love you."

PART 3

Generation Z: The Future— "What comes next?"

"I continue to believe that if children are given the necessary tools to succeed, they will succeed beyond their wildest dreams!"

—DAVID VITTER, FORMER US SENATOR

CHAPTER 10

Kenny, the Future

Kenny's graduation stuck in his mind like it was only yesterday. After working so hard to master his lessons, he finally passed the requirements to move forward. He was a quick student and learning from memory came easy to him. Demonstrating his new skills was a little more challenging. From a very early age he had learned to interface with a screen and keyboard. Having to perform in the physical world was something that made him a little uncomfortable. He thought about the silky gown and funny graduation hat that he was wearing. They were so unlike anything he had worn before. He had to consciously think about keeping his head held high so that the cap did not fall off.

Kenny took his place in line along with the other graduates. He was nervous about being in front of all those people, yet he was excited about his accomplishment. He knew his dad was proud of him too. He scanned the audience as he approached the curtain. He saw his dad in the sixth row with his iPhone held out in front of him, just like all of the other friends and relatives. Kenny knew that within a few minutes almost everyone he knew would be watching him step up to receive his diploma. He knew how quickly videos could be distributed via the internet. That was how you shared events like this.

When the director called out his name, Kenny sheepishly walked to the center of the stage. The director and his teacher both shook his hand as he was handed the diploma. "We are so proud of you, Kenny. You have worked so hard to learn all of the fundamentals. We know you will make a wonderful first-grader next year." Kenny's family gathered round him and snapped pictures for Snapchat. Everyone was delighted to pose next to the five-year-old and smile while taking a selfie. Thumbs floated across the keyboards as pictures were uploaded and shared around the world. Soon they were headed back to their small home in the Little Havana district of Miami, Florida. Kenny was excited about the big celebration with family and friends.

Kenny's father, Christian, had come to the United States on a student visa in the early 1980s. The University of Miami was a melting pot of cultures from all over Florida and the Caribbean. Christian, or Chris, easily fit in to the energy and flow of college life there. He soon learned that he could keep his visa renewed as long as he never completed a degree in a particular field of study. Chris's ploy was to take courses in a major field and then switch to a new one as he neared the requirements for graduation. It was hard to attend classes and work enough hours to be able to afford his lifestyle, but Chris was used to hard work. Even this busy life was easier than it had been on his native island of Trinidad.

In March of 1992 Chris was sitting in a coffee shop on Calle Ocho when a waitress there caught his eye. He made is way over and introduced himself. Selena was two years older than Chris but had a very youthful air to her. Her natural smile and graceful way of moving made Chris's heart beat faster. She evidently was just as attracted to him as he was to her. From day one, they were inseparable. Selena was the mother of two other children. Alejandra was just a toddler, born in 1988. Roberto had been named after his father and was born in 1985. Selena hadn't seen Roberto

Sr. in over a year. They were never married. He just didn't come home one night, and she had never heard from him again. She worked hard to care for her two little ones and provide a small but comfortable home for them.

Christian and Selena Lara were married at St. Michael the Archangel church in June of that year. Chris dedicated himself to providing for Selena and her children. He accepted them and cared for them as his own. He was finally able to become a United States citizen in October of that year. No more attending classes just to remain in the country. Their new baby boy, Kendon Lara, arrived in August of 1998.

As a little boy growing up in a blended family in a culturally rich neighborhood, Kendon was exposed to a plethora of activities. Street sports and ethnic festivals seemed like everyday occurrences. Attending church each week was a requirement. School and a good education were a must. His older siblings loved their little brother and spent time with him constantly, playing with him and trying to make him laugh. Even though they were older than him, he loved to be with them. As children of the millennial generation, they were attached to their handheld technology. From that early age, Kendon was drawn to explore the possibilities of it. It didn't take him long to see that their phones were an important part of their lives. He was still very young when he started asking his dad when he could have one of his own. Chris told him that would happen when he was a little older. In the meantime, Kendon could use Chris's new smartphone to play games.

Kendon preferred the American style of his name, Kenny, instead of the formal style he would have been known in his father's Trinidad. The family didn't have much, but they had everything they needed, including a home computer. Kenny loved playing games on it. He immersed himself into learning everything possible and was soon an internet guru. Chris and Selena would often ask him to look things up for them as he was much faster and effective in his searches. Kenny worked hard on his studies as Chris demanded. He was an overachiever and Chris knew that he had the opportunity to follow in his footsteps at Miami.

In September of 2006, as the family was sitting down to dinner, a news story came on the television remembering the 911 disaster. The family entered into a conversation reliving the events of that day. Kenny sat and listened. He didn't remember anything about it firsthand. He was well aware of what had happened through YouTube videos and Google searches. But he could see the emotion welling up in his dad's eyes as he talked about the country he had grown to love so much being attacked in such a vicious manner. Kenny felt strongly about the situation but didn't feel that sense of emotional connection to it. *I guess that's just another way that I am different from Alex and Bobby,* he thought.

Kenny loved his older siblings. He watched them continually and gradually became aware of what they needed in their lives to make them feel prepared for adulthood. Bobby was graduating high school that spring and was planning on studying history at Florida Southern University in the fall. He had been a good high school student and had won a few small scholarships. Still Chris and Selena didn't have the funds to pay for the rest of his education. Like so many others in his class, he would be applying for student loans to get him through. Alex would soon be going down that same path.

Little did they know that just two years into the future, America would plunge into a deep economic recession. Chris would lose his job. Selena would find work to help out. The family would struggle. Bobby would leave school to help make ends meet. The student loans that he had accumulated would become a weight around his neck that would nearly drown him. Kenny wanted to help as well. He had the reputation as a smart kid who could be trusted. He soon found odd jobs that brought the family a few dollars here and there. He liked being able to contribute. Chris told him to keep one out of every three dollars that he earned. Kenny carefully put each one of them in a cigar box that he got down at the corner store. Having money, even a little, set aside gave him a sense of security. He hated to see his brother have such a hard time paying back his debt. Kenny vowed that he would start saving money for his own education early so that he could avert the same situation. From that time on, Kenny would prefer to save his money instead of spend it. Kenny would carry the lessons he learned during this time with him throughout his life. As he grew through his teen years, he was constantly looking for work that would allow him to have things he wanted yet have money set aside in case he needed it.

By 2012, Kenny's interest in technology had grown significantly. It seemed like there was a new application coming out every month. He finally made the decision to use some of his savings to invest in a new smartphone, yet he struggled with taking money from his savings. He turned to his father for advice. Chris and Kenny sat and discussed the balance between having money and spending some on something Kenny wanted. Chris had lived through tough economic times and had learned many financial lessons the hard way. He tried to advise Kenny on how to make a choice, but he took care to never tell him what to do. He had learned valuable lessons while helping raise Bobby and Alex. They now struggled with accepting the accountability for their own decisions. Chris didn't want Kenny to go down that road. He knew that teaching Kenny the value of seeing the outcomes of decisions would help him throughout his life. He, like so many parents, had made too many decisions for Kenny's older siblings. One day, Kenny asked his dad why he didn't get all of the things he had seen Bobby and Alex get as kids.

"Good question, son," Chris said. "As parents, we learn pretty much as we go. Sure, there are books and videos that want to tell us everything they think we should know, but real learning comes from experience. There was a time not long ago when parents felt like they needed to provide everything for their kids. They thought that if they made everyone equal, there would be a great feeling of inclusion and worth with all of the kids. Little did they know that this would not solve their challenges in being prepared for the real world. In fact, it might have made things worse for them. You know that feeling you get when you have worked hard to cut someone's lawn and it looks really good? Then when they hand you the money that you have literally sweated to earn and you see the smile on their face, you get a deep sense of pride in what you have accomplished?"

"Sure do," Kenny replied. "Sometimes, as tired as I am, I want to go right into the next job. It kind of energizes me and makes me want to do more."

"Absolutely! You know that I love Bobby and Alex with all of my heart. There isn't anything I wouldn't do for them. But I have also learned a lot by watching them grow up. They don't often get that warm fuzzy feeling that comes from accomplishment. It's not them; it's just what they learned from the way we raised them. There is a lot you can learn as well from watching them too. Selena and I want you to be absolutely prepared for your future. Sometimes that means helping you earn instead of just giving you things. Think of it like this. We don't give you everything because we love you so much."

It was about this time that Kenny was introduced to something that would change his life. When he was a freshman in high school, his school introduced a program to which Kenny was instantly attracted. His science teacher, Sean McCandless[7] launched the first STEM (Science, Technology, Engineering, and Mathematics) program at his school. The students who were interested in hands-on learning in advanced technical fields would get together every Thursday afternoon for workshops. Kenny had always liked Mr. Mac, as the student called him. Mr. Mac also cared deeply for his students. He understood that teaching was more about challenging them to find their own learning pathways instead of just providing them with answers to write on a test. STEM was all about experiential learning. Kenny loved it and couldn't get enough. It was Mr. Mac who first introduced him to unmanned aerial vehicles, more

---

[7]   The character of Sean McCandless is based on the real life of Sean McSeehy. Sean is an Engineering teacher at Choctawhatchee High school in Fort Walton Beach Florida where he heads the STEM program. Sean is also CEO of the US Drone Team. He is instrumental in helping kids develop skills and abilities that will be valuable to them in their professional careers. More can be learned about his work at www.droneteamchallenge.com.

commonly known as drones. Kenny loved watching the machines soar and hover, but he was even more intrigued with understanding how they worked. It was Mr. Mac however who created the deeper interest for Kenny. When Kenny wanted to learn how to fly drones, Mr. Mac told him that he would need to learn the concepts of how drones worked. When Kenny wanted to buy his own drone, Mr. Mac encouraged him to design his own and helped him manufacture the parts on a 3D printer. When Kenny wanted to compete, Mr. Mac helped him master flying through virtual visual technology. And when Kenny mastered drones, Mr. Mac encouraged him to become a mentor to others who were less experienced than him. Kenny's dad was still his counselor in life, but it was Mr. Mac who made Kenny want to become an engineer. Mr. Mac taught him that most all STEM principles can be found and applied in today's UAV/Drone Technology. Having a vision of the future and what the world might look like in ten years helped Kenny decide where he wanted to go in his life. It was Mr. Mac's influence and his own dad's council that led him into civil engineering.

Through Mr. Mac's STEM class, Kenny made friends with others who shared his interest in drones. They made a great team, constantly encouraging each other to think of new improvements in creating their individual drones. Kenny was surprised that although they shared a common interest, they were also very different. They frequently talked about their home lives. Kenny liked hearing their stories. He became aware that although they grew up in homes somewhat similar to his, there were still a lot of differences. He realized how fortunate he was to have a dad and mom who paid such close attention to him. They also talked about things that were going on in the world. Their conversations about current events covered a broad scale. They talked about the weather disasters like Hurricane Sandy in New York, the end of the Mayan calendar, and nuclear testing in North Korea. Kenny was fascinated with Google's new deep learning machine. He had never even heard of artificial intelligence, and now it was becoming a reality. He and his friends spent a lot of time thinking about applications for it and how it could change their future.

One of Kenny's favorite times came in the middle of his sophomore year. Mr. Mac gave the class a challenge that shaped Kenny's thinking in more ways than one. Mr. Mac divided the class into teams of four. Their assignment was to design and create their own drones. The most exciting part was that they would have a flying competition at the end of the project. Mr. Mac was masterful in designing the project to provide maximum hands-on learning for the teams and to provide them with an opportunity to collaborate on both design and implementation. Kenny was elated. His team consisted of Antonio, Olivia, Michael, and himself. Michael was in his class, Antonio was a year older, and Olivia was a year younger than him. The challenge would be divided into individual learning opportunities. They would research the design of the team's drone and build it themselves using the tools Mr. Mac had acquired. They would also go through a series of curricula to teach them about the principles of flight with unmanned aerial vehicles, how to fly drones through virtual simulation, how to use drone mounted cameras in the first-person view, how to program their drones from scratch, and, finally, how to mentor others. Mr. Mac knew that this last step would deepen and enrich their knowledge and ability while creating new relationships with others. Their work on the project would be the first step in developing these communication skills.

The team met the next Thursday afternoon at their weekly STEM group session. They were one of six teams taking on the challenge. There was a lot of energy and excitement, but also some trepidation about where and how to begin. They talked about their background experiences and areas of personal interest that would lead them to success. Antonio had previously been in a similar challenge with robots and knew how to create a plan. Michael was a dedicated virtual gamer. Kenny was surprised to hear that Michael's parents gave him unlimited time to play online games at home, but he figured that was what made him good at what he did. Kenny thought that Michael's experience would be valuable when it came to the virtual simulation. This was Olivia's first time working on a team project, let alone one that was actually a competition. Kenny felt that the work ethic that his dad had developed in him would help to keep everyone focused. They exchanged ideas throughout that first session and finally landed on their takeaway. They would each research unmanned aerial vehicles and learn as much as possible about design. Their objective for the next meeting would be to agree on a design and create a basic project plan to begin the process of creating their own competition drone. Kenny left with his own personal plan. He would pour through every YouTube video he could find and catalog the best pieces from each one. He was confident that he could prove himself a leader on the team.

The team reconvened the next Thursday. Antonio had found an experienced drone flier in Miami and had convinced his parents to take him to meet him. His interview with that flier provided numerous valuable ideas. Olivia had done some reading on the principles of drone flight but didn't have a lot to contribute. The team understood and was empathetic to her since this was her first project of this type. They knew she would become more comfortable as they moved through the project. Michael excitedly shared some of the scenarios he had experienced in one of his combat games. There was one in particular that used drones as weapons in a war simulation. He had become rather adept at using them to conquer his opponents in the game. The team had trouble understanding how that would relate to what they were doing, but they listened respectfully. When Kenny's time came, he shared the things he had learned from YouTube. He also showed the team some of the more pertinent clips he had downloaded. Everyone agreed that the ideas would give them a strong starting point. They excitedly moved into the project plan phase, everyone that is, except Michael. He seemed to be hurt that his ideas weren't as accepted as others. He withdrew from active participation and merely listened as the plan was created.

The next week, they drafted their plan for Mr. Mac's approval. They presented it to him as a team. Mr. Mac gave them feedback on their design, approved their plan, and gave them access to the tools they would need to begin building their drone. Mr. Mac noticed that Michael didn't seem to share the same level of enthusiasm and asked him if he was OK.

"Sure," Michael replied. "I just have some things going on at home that are distracting me." Kenny made a mental note to ask Michael if there was anything he could do to help.

As the weeks went by and the project progressed, Kenny noticed a change in Michael's behavior. He missed a couple of the Thursday classes, and when he was there, he appeared to be easily agitated. Kenny asked Michael if he was OK. Michael once again told him that he had "some stuff going on at home." Kenny had always talked easily with his parents and grandparents. They had always given him good council. He asked Michael if he had talked to his dad about what was bothering him. Michael responded, "My dad isn't interested in me. When I try to talk to him, he tells me that he is busy. He tells me to go play my video games or talk to my online friends. Sometimes I feel like he doesn't care if I am there or not. He and my mom fight all the time. I wish they would just get a divorce." Kenny was saddened by this. He decided that he needed to talk to his dad about what he should do to help Michael.

When Kenny explained the situation to his dad, Chris listened attentively. Chris knew Kenny well and always knew the best advice to give him in his life, but hearing about Kenny's friend was a different story. Chris helped Kenny understand that other people sometimes chose to run their homes and families differently. He reminded Kenny how he and Selena made it a point to be there for the kids, how they always tried to do the best things for them even if it might seem to be a harder road. He helped Kenny understand how Michael's situation appeared to be different from that, and he encouraged Kenny to try to be the best friend possible to Michael. He also told Kenny that he might want to talk to Mr. Mac about it, as Mr. Mac knew Michael better. Kenny left the conversation feeling a little better but still very concerned for his friend.

206

When the team's first-generation drone was completed, they decided that Michael would be the first to give it the test flight. They knew his gaming experience would translate to the actual flight and were excited as they presented the offer to him. They were surprised when he declined to be the test pilot. Michael's reason was that he didn't feel worthy of that responsibility. Olivia had really blossomed in her knowledge and contribution to the team, so they offered the test flight to her. She beamed as she took the controller and lifted the drone off of the ground for the first time. Kenny and Antonio applauded and cheered. Michael disappeared to the corner of the room and slipped out a side door. When Kenny noticed this, he realized that he needed to talk with Mr. Mac.

Mr. Mac listened to the story Kenny told him. He too had seen changes in Michael's behavior and was concerned. As a teacher, he was required to be supportive but not take action unless he believed there could be a danger to the student. Mr. Mac thanked Kenny for his concern for his friend and for all he did to try to help Michael. He assured Kenny that he would take the appropriate steps to help Michael in any way possible. Kenny left the meeting feeling a little like he might have betrayed his friend's confidence but also that he did the right thing in talking to Mr. Mac. He later found out that his intervention with Mr. Mac probably saved Michael's life. He learned that Michael had sunk deep into depression and had been having thoughts of ending his own life. Fortunately, professionals were able to get him the help he needed to begin to get his life back on track.

The flight competition was held on a Saturday morning in May in Domino Park. It was a series of "fly through" obstacles of varying size and height. All six teams were represented and had their best pilot man the controller. Olivia did an outstanding job, but they still finished in third place. Their unmanned aerial vehicle did, however, win the best design award. The cover story on the competition's Facebook page showed Olivia proudly holding the drone. Clearly emblazoned on the side was the name "Michael's Marvel." They had unanimously decided to christen it after the absent member of their team in his honor.

Over the next couple of years, Kenny would have many more things to contemplate. He knew the United States was becoming an increasingly less safe place. News of the Boston marathon bombing, the Baltimore riots following the Freddie Gray incident, and the rise of ISIS made him more acutely aware of his own safety and security. He knew that there were increasingly more risks in the cyber world as well. The kids frequently talked to Mr. Mac about these things. Mr. Mac had a way of helping them understand the risks that come with easy access to information on the internet. He also helped them to explore ideas about how they might make a difference in making the world a safer place. All of the things happening, and how quickly the world was changing, affected some of the kids differently than Kenny. He was glad that he could always go to his family to talk through things that were bothering him. A few of his friends, however, didn't seem to handle the changes as well as he did. He saw them begin to become introverted and depressed. He wished he could help them, but he didn't know how to do that.

Kenny graduated from high school with honors in May of 2016. Although he had been accepted into the University of Florida's engineering program and was planning on moving to Gainesville in the fall, he wasn't convinced that civil engineering was the career path for him. He still loved drone work and had become a master pilot. He was also a mentor to several of the newer kids in Mr. Mac's program. His dad once again became his counselor and helped him with his decision.

His dad told him, "I have an old friend who runs an engineering company up in Virginia. Maybe I can get him to let you come up for a few days and see how the engineering business runs. Sound like something you might be interested in doing?"

Kenny arrived at Sawgrass Engineering on a Tuesday morning. Christian's friend Bill Thomas met him at the door. Bill walked Kenny around and introduced him to the CEO, Nancy, his team of senior engineers, and most of the other staff. Bill turned him over to Eric Waddell to show him the software they used. Kenny was somewhat familiar with AutoCAD from his time with Mr. Mac. He was surprised to see that the engineering field was still using that as a primary platform. He wondered why no one had come up with something more modern. "I guess civil engineering isn't that modern and progressive," he thought to himself. Bill took him out to lunch, and they talked about the kind of work Sawgrass did. Kenny was surprised at all of the details, deadlines, and meetings required to complete a site design project. He thought the municipal work looked pretty boring. His mind wandered back to the excitement of building and flying drones. After lunch, Bill had him spend the afternoon with Ben Peterson to learn some about the overall management of engineering projects. At the end of the day, Nancy and Bill talked with Kenny about his experience. Kenny had a hard time hiding his disappointment. However, his parents had taught him to be kind and he kept a smile on his face and happiness in his voice. He was pretty sure, though, that engineering wasn't for him. By the end of his second day at Sawgrass, Kenny knew what he wanted to do with his career, and what he didn't want to do.

In September of that year, Kenny was enrolled in Embry-Riddle Aeronautical University in Daytona Beach. He was pursuing a bachelor of science in unmanned aircraft systems. His passion of flying UAVs soon led him to begin thinking of innovative designs and applications. As he studied, he kept a journal of ideas where drones would provide value to existing business. Kenny realized that UAV was the future of aeronautics. He was confident that his educational pathway was in a field that would provide him with meaningful work for the rest of his life.

If Kenny had a crystal ball and could look into his future, he would see himself holding a master's of science in unmanned and autonomous systems engineering. He would be the holder of three patents in the field of drone technology. He would use his entrepreneurial skills to create a mapping program using drones. The practical application of this would ironically be used in civil engineering. Kenny's drones would fly over a prospective job site, use ground penetrating radar and 3D scanning software to identify underground impediments, map the field, and draw plans for all required utilities and site preparation. Eventually he would be employed as a contractor for numerous civil engineering companies, Sawgrass Engineering among them. He would enjoy a long and lucrative career as an innovator and mentor, all within the field of unmanned autonomous vehicle technology.

What has shaped Generation Z:

- 911 (Although they don't have firsthand recollection, the worldwide change following 911 has impacted their world.)
- The Iraq wars; war on terror both at home and abroad
- Natural disasters related to climate change: Hurricanes Katrina, Sandy, Harvey, Irma, Jose, Maria, Ike, Rita, Florence, and Michael; Haiti earthquake; Indonesian tsunami
- The recession of 2008
- Smart handheld devices; YouTube; virtual social networking
- Apple iPad
- Consumer robotics; artificial intelligence; internet of things; 3D printers; drones
- Rise of ISIS/security concerns
- Social sharing (Uber, Lyft, Airbnb)
- Legality/acceptance of same-sex marriage
- Blurring of gender identification
- Human rights issues; protests and movements
- Absence of political collaboration
- Web-connected video devices exceed the global population (2017)
- Wearable technology (iWatch, Fitbit, Garmin)
- Voice interactive devices (Siri, Alexis, Ok Google)

What they need in the workplace as they enter the job market:

- Digital media vs. paper; all reading is done online
- Total connectivity; portable devices are an extension of themselves; internet of things in the workplace; 5g speed everywhere; using wearable technology at work
- Pragmatic, tech-savvy environment
- Video communication and learning
- Individually designed workspace; multiple screens is the norm
- Digital privacy; security is an issue
- Accessible internal applications
- Trusted mentors
- Health-conscious environment
- Handheld and wearable devices are everything; total connectivity through them
- Salary is important; they expect to make $200K/year; they choose salary over work-life balance
- Communication through social media vs. face-to-face
- Comprehensive individual development opportunities

Work ethic and values:

- They are 100% digitally connected. They have never known life without it. Among ages 13–22, 95% have smartphones; 55% use them more than 5 hours/day. Wide usage of video and conversational interfaces (Siri/Alexa).[8]
- They are excellent multitaskers; used to working on multiple screens
- They have never known life without cultural diversity

---

[8]   Heather Watson, "How Obsessed Is Gen Z with Mobile Technology?" The Center for Generational Kinetics, Accessed September 1, 2019, https://genhq.com/how-obsessed-is-gen-z-with-mobile-technology/.

- They tend to reach out to grandparents and parents for advice vs. third party
- They are learning from their millennial siblings (younger) and parents (older); they want their lives to be different
- They plan for higher education without student debt
- They want to work their way through; they want to make an impact through their career
- They want to plan their own future
- They have a high incidence rate of loneliness and depression from being 100% digitally connected
- They are stressed. 58% say they have at least moderate stress. Only 53% say their lives have a purpose. They spend a lot of time looking for ways to relieve that stress.[9]
- Privacy/safety are issues (internet piracy, neighborhood violence)
- Interracial and blended families are normal
- They want to make a difference in the world (and at work)
- Financial security is important; they value salary over work-life balance
- They craft their own personal style (uniqueness is important)
- They embrace artificial intelligence and robotics
- Multicultural heritage (52% of people under 18 are Caucasian vs. 75% for boomers)[10]
- Where millennials grew up in a time of change, Generation Zers see all of those changes as normal
- Where the internet brings them in touch with cool people and things, they feel they might be lacking that connection personally
- They embrace gender blurring; less than 50% identify as completely heterosexual[11]

---

9   Ben Graham, "Five Big Differences Between Millennials and Gen Z that You Need to Know," Medium, March 7, 2018, https://medium.com/writers-guild/five-big-differences-between-millennials-and-gen-z-that-you-need-to-know-fdefb607fc41.
10   Ibid.
11   Ibid.

- They use social media less than millennials (and differently)
- They use Instagram to follow brands
- They use Snapchat to communicate with friends (quick hit)
- They use Facebook for news (user groups) or to see what their parents are saying about them
- College is not the only answer (technology and trades are options). They realize that there can be more money in careers that require human contact, those that cannot be replaced by artificial intelligence and robotics.
- Authentic experiences are more important than material items (gift-giving/rewards and recognition)
- They are opportunists; keep them engaged and developing or risk losing them
- They want to make a difference and are willing to work hard to make that happen
- They seek influence from older, more experienced people

CHAPTER 11

Generation Z as a "Throwback" Generation

Generation Z is just beginning to enter the workforce from a non-skilled level. The members of this generation who have chosen continuing education (college, technical, or trades) are still finishing up their post-secondary education. As such, we don't have a lot of data around how they will actually perform in the workplace. We do, however, have some interesting facts that help to predict their behavior. As we have learned from our generational journey throughout this book, attributes are categorized for generations based on more than the years in which they were born. Each generation's pattern behavior is shaped by factors beyond those years. Among these are major events, social changes, and familial influences.

In 1991 William Strauss and Neil Howe, in their books *Generations*

(1991)[12] and *The Fourth Turning* (1997),[13] theorized that there were predictable generational cycles throughout American history dating back to 1584. They speculated that generational behaviors repeated in four predictable cycles. They labeled these cycles as "Idealist," "Reactive," "Civic," and Adaptive." They also wrote that each generation was marked by a triggering event, or "turning point" that defined that generation. If we follow their line of thinking, we can reasonably predict that Generation Z should be similar in thoughts and behaviors to the traditionalist generation.

Whether or not Strauss' and Howe's theory holds true for Generation Z is yet to be determined. However, there are numerous behavior-shaping factors and similarities between Generation Z and the traditionalist generation that may indicate that this could be a "throwback" generation. Among them are:

- Both came of age during a time of economic crisis and recovery
  - Great Depression (1929)
  - Great recession (2008)

- Both came of age during worldwide conflicts
  - World War II
  - Global war on terror

- Both experienced the change of commonly accepted marital values
  - Marrying outside of your heritage, religion, native language
  - Marrying outside of your race, ethnicity, and same gender

---

[12]   William Strauss and Neil Howe, *Generations: The History of America's Future, 1584–2069* (Quill, 1992).

[13]   William Strauss and Neil Howe, *The Fourth Turning: An American Prophecy—What the Cycles of History Tell Us About America's Next Rendezvous with Destiny* (New York: Three Rivers Press, 1997).

216

- Both came of age on the cusp of business/trades changes
  - Power tools, electronics, early computing
  - Robotics, unmanned aerial vehicles, artificial intelligence

- Both came of age during a time of technology change
  - Commercialism of cars, flight, television
  - Smartphones, integrated wireless technology, internet of things

- Both experienced a breakdown in national political trust
  - McCarthyism
  - Bipartisan stalemate and fake political news

- Both demonstrate a high level of resourcefulness
  - Made things at home
  - "Hacks"

- Both are highly visible learners
  - Influence of television
  - Online videos (59% say YouTube is the #1 way they prefer to learn)[14]

- Both are primarily face-to-face communicators
  - Handshakes and conversation
  - Snapchat, Instagram

- The world was/is a risky place for both
  - Cold War with Russia
  - Terrorism

---

[14] Beyond Millennials: The Next Generation of Learners," Pearson, Global Research and Insights, August 2018, https://www.pearson.com/content/dam/one-dot-com/one-dot-com/global/Files/news/news-annoucements/2018/The-Next-Generation-of-Learners_final.pdf.

- Both are "savers" over "spenders" (due to influence of first bullet point)
- Both tend to seek advice from family first
- Both prefer to "play it safe" (risk averse)
- Both seek a "comfort" lifestyle
- Both saw traditionally accepted values be replaced
- Both had/have great optimism for the future
- Both planned their careers to jobs/roles that were predicted to be in demand
- Both take a practical approach (self-defined) to their lives vs. an idealistic (planned by others) approach
- Both place a high value on family units (it's cool to be tight with mom and dad)

Most researchers who are studying Generation Z have great optimism for how they will perform in the workplace. This generation is educated, resourceful, and intuitive. They have a strong entrepreneurial spirit. They have learned from observing their older millennial friends and family. They are acutely aware of things like college debt, lack of proper preparation for careers, and upcoming technology. They are planning their lives to be high wage earners and are willing to put work over life to achieve that. They expect to reach C-Suite level and crave the development it will take to get there. They are opportunists and want to make an impact through their career. They filter information quickly and are used to working on numerous items simultaneously. Overall, they are predicted to be strong contributors to the business world. The business world needs to be ready for them.

CHAPTER 12

Bringing It All Together

Generational diversity in the workplace is an opportunity to intertwine the assets of employees from different generations to achieve dynamic outcomes. Let's consider a generational recipe for success in the workplace.

Great recipes result from quality ingredients blended effectively together to produce a desired outcome. Each generation produces qualities and assets that are central to the equation for success. As was illustrated in our generational examples, the traditionalists were hardworking employees with determined spirits, boomers became innovators, Generation Xers incorporated advancements in technology, millennials provided creative alternatives, and Generation Zers are likely to usher in a new era such as the use of artificial intelligence. Each generational ingredient provides value when combined in the proper proportion. Too much or too little of any ingredient will affect the outcome. For example, a group of creative thinkers without planners and doers will never be anything more than a concept. A fleet of exceptionally designed drones without operating instructions or operators are destined to become dust collectors. It is the effective blending of the ingredients that produces a desired outcome.

Blending is a process associated with a methodology and an initiator. To create the recipe the initiator must clearly understand the method. To have a recipe that can be duplicated, the creator of the recipe must effectively communicate the methodology to those who will be assembling and combining the ingredients. As specified earlier, effective communication is defined as "the message sent must be equal to message received." The most brilliant of chefs will struggle to duplicate a recipe written in a language they don't comprehend. In the workplace, if I don't understand the technological expectations it is unlikely I will properly employ them. For most recipes, success depends on adding the ingredients in the right amount at the right time for the ingredients to blend compatibly. For any given recipe, there may be several different instructions for blending based on the equipment or resources to be used. For example, blending by hand is considerably different in expectations than blending using a professional mixer. The specific timeline for one process is likely to be completely different from another process to obtain the highest quality outcome.

In the workplace, blending the talents and experience of employees from different generations requires careful consideration. A project initiator needs to clearly understand the strengths and limitations of each team member to determine how they can effectively work together. Expectations must be clearly communicated using techniques which result in all members developing a common frame of reference. Each member working on the project needs to be aware of the parameters for completing their portion of the project and why their adherence to the plan and schedule is essential to the outcome. Groups composed of employees from different generations are likely to respond to different motivators and enhancers. Mentoring may be necessary to help team members adapt to new technology. Meetings may be used to generate enthusiasm and to collectively track progress. Social events can facilitate group cohesion. Incentives might be used to expedite completion of the project. When the employees and their talents effectively blend together, differences become assets.

Considerable attention in this book has been devoted to identifying and understanding generational differences. To effectively blend the generations, it will be helpful to also understand the commonalities of the human experience. Most obvious is the biological patterns of human growth and development. Basic biology has been consistent for centuries across geographic, racial, and cultural parameters. The processes of respiration, circulation, digestion, neural function, genetics, and reproduction follow similar patterns whether a person was born B.C. or A.D. As we explored in reviewing Erikson's stages of development, there are patterns for personality and character development. Acquisition of knowledge (learning) occurs in a pattern associated with brain development and level of capacity. Even Maslow's Hierarchy of Need has universal application from basic survival to social inclusion and ultimately esteem. So from a human standpoint, there is very little difference between a traditionalist and Gen Zer and every generation in between. The differences between generations are created by the social and cultural experiences the person encounters in development. If the social experiences are similar, the result is generally similar behavior and attitudes.

Consider the similarities of our five generational examples: traditionalist Walt, baby boomer Nancy, Gen Xer Bill, millennial Ashlee, and Gen Zer Kenny.

- Each was raised with parental concern for their welfare and all developed positive family relationships.
- Each faced environmental obstacles which helped them persevere through difficult adult challenges.
- Each witnessed others who struggled to adjust to their life circumstance and all developed a desire to support and encourage others.

- Each was raised to consider education important and all of them became achievers.
- Each had role models for working hard to support a family and all found success in the workplace.
- Each pursued personal goals, and all experienced esteem through accomplishment.

In essence, there are likely far more things that are similar about individuals from different generations than there are differences. Often the process is the same, however, the mechanisms vary. Consider these generational ranges:

Process	Range
Communication	Rotary dial telephone to Twitter
Technology	Party-line phones to Siri
Family Constellation	Nuclear family to alternative family
Child rearing	Candyland to Candy Crush
Affiliation	Nationalism to Globalism
Value System	Moral code to universal acceptance
Personal Needs	A chicken in every pot to a cell phone in every pocket

Even though circumstances change continually, basic human dynamics remain similar. One consistency across generations is that when an individual enters the workplace, they intend to experience a benefit. A second factor is that each worker from any generation will have expectations that are unique to them. So how do we bring the generations together in a workplace? Success in the workplace is the result of intention rather than wishful thinking. Intent requires direction and energy. The style of this book is learning through storytelling. Let's consider a classic story, *The Wizard of Oz*.

It would surprise me if you haven't seen the movie, *The Wizard of Oz*. If not, download it today. The story line is that a young girl gets caught in a tumultuous storm and lands in a strange place, only to find herself with an overwhelming challenge. (Sounds like the first day of work at a new job, doesn't it?) The challenge is so overwhelming she believes she needs a magical solution to overcome it. On her journey along the yellow brick road to find a magical solution, she encounters three characters all with dilemmas of their own: a brainless scarecrow, an empty tin man, and a cowardly lion. They all decide a magical solution would be good for them, so they join her on the journey. Of course, there is a villain, a domineering witch with a shoe fetish. The hopeful foursome, anticipating a magic fix, get an audience with the wizard, only to have him complicate their problems by giving them a challenge: in order to earn their desired wish, they must destroy his problem—the witch. The witch captures the girl, then the trio rescues the girl with their caring, clever plan, and courage. All beat overwhelming odds to escape, while accidently destroying the villain along the way. Throw in a few flying monkeys and a little dog that figures out all the problems before the characters do and you have a great story.

I hope that you are wondering what this has to do with blending generations to create a successful workplace. The relevance is in how the story ends. It turns out that the wizard is not all-wise. He's just a clever entrepreneur who turned a problem into an opportunity by understanding how people think. He recognizes that the scarecrow only thinks he's not capable because his intelligence hasn't been validated by others. He helps the tin man understand that it is his desire to love that feeds his passion rather than needing to be loved. He enables the lion to discover that courage lies in believing in oneself rather than the ability to intimidate others. He helps the young girl realize that she doesn't need magic to achieve her goals and that she needs to believe in herself and put forth the effort to pursue it. There is one final caveat. In the final scene, the girl discovers that the obstacles in the story were not real. Instead, they were in her imagination. What insights does the trip to Oz offer?

- The introduction of a new challenge can seem daunting, particularly if you are not sure it is achievable.
- If you have an idea of where you want to end up and why you want to end up there, you are motivated to begin the journey.
- To put together an effective team, you need to be interested in the characteristics of the team members looking for both abilities and potential abilities.
- All team members need to want to end up at the same place, even if for different reasons.
- Wishful thinking will not solve the challenges. Intent and dedication will lead to productivity.
- Intelligence, confidence, and passion will be required to overcome obstacles.
- It is important that each individual take ownership for their role in the process and appreciate their contribution to the outcome.

Success in the workforce is the result of intention rather than wishful thinking. Intention requires direction and energy. For humans, that direction is provided by leaders. As infants, our care givers provide direction. As development progresses, additional leaders emerge. In considering leadership and generational differences, let's examine the elements that converted four characters from very different backgrounds into an effective team.

1. Where were they going? The girl was headed along the yellow brick road to Oz and convinced those she came across along the way to go there with her.

2. Why did they want to go there? They all expected to get something that they wanted.
3. What did they expect to get when they got there? Each character was seeking something different, but they all believed having what they were after would fulfill their life.
4. What did they need to get them there? They had to believe it was possible. They needed a plan and direction. They needed determination and continued encouragement.
5. Who was their audience? The wizard (who required that they meet his expectations before he was willing to provide what they wanted).
6. What challenges/obstacles did they expect to encounter along the way? Lack of hope, fire, water, and disappointment were the obvious obstacles. What they didn't expect was sleep-inducing poppies, flying monkeys, a sinister control freak, and another challenge from the wizard. Each challenge they overcame increased their belief that they could conquer the next.

Our story provides a spectrum of leadership. A girl who becomes an unsuspecting leader, a witch who wants to rule over and control others, a dog who was routinely pointing the way, three supposedly inept characters who discovered their potential as self-leaders, and a wizard, pretending to be a leader, who understands how to make the people he works with successful.

When we think of leadership in the workplace, we generally think about the person in charge of the group. A basic aspect of effective leadership is understanding who you are leading. Similar to the operation of a piece of equipment, the better the operator understands how the equipment works and what it is capable of producing, the more efficiently the equipment can be used or repaired if something were to go awry. When the components are people, the better the leader understands the team member's abilities and personalities, the more effectively they can be facilitated to achieve a common goal. This is particularly important when the employees have different generational perspectives. Recall in chapter 5 the struggles Wyatt Wontwerk had in leading his team because he didn't completely understand their perspective. Often the first step in effective leadership is helping employees to better understand their potential as self-leaders.

Let's revisit the questions raised above as elements of self-leadership.

1. Where am I going?
2. Why do I want to go there?
3. What do I expect when I get there?
4. What do I need to get there?
5. Who is my audience?
6. Which challenges/obstacles do I expect to encounter along the way?

The fundamental element in the workplace is the individual employee. Surprisingly few employees consider their responsibility as self-leaders. As a self-leader, when you evaluate your attitude and performance in the workplace how much consideration have you given to the questions listed above? If your answer is a considerable amount, it is likely that you are quite productive. Let's take a closer look at self-leadership and how it contributes to productivity in the workplace.

The first three questions regarding the elements to leadership relate to objectives associated with the work experience. You might wonder why the first question is "Where am I going?" vs. "What do I want?" The reason: *want* is an outcome and *going* is a process. For example, I want to earn six figures or I want to be the boss. Is that all you want? Are you finished with work when you get what you want? Will you experience actualization earning six figures or being the boss? Will you want something more after you get what you think you want? The work experience is a process, a journey where we are our own leaders.

"Where are you going?" implies direction rather than an endpoint. It refers to the journey that is the work experience. Where you want to go parallels the reaction of children in response to what excites them. When I grow up, I want to be a doctor, lawyer, or chef. The journey is heading to a place that we think will solve our troubles and make us happy and fulfilled. This is our vision of Oz.

"Why do I want to go there?" is the fulfillment of expectations. It's what motivates us to start and continue the journey. For example, I want to feel accomplished, prove my worth, test the limits of my capabilities, or achieve status. Clearly the girl on her way to Oz wasn't hoping to encounter a dastardly villain, be captured, or have her life threatened. She merely wanted to go home where she felt she belonged.

What I expect are the milestones I want to achieve, tangible and intangible payoffs for making the journey. Tangibles may include money, recognition, power, and prestige. Intangibles, such as a sense of value, self-pride, belongingness, and esteem, are also important in motivating the effort to complete the journey. What many in the work-life journey do not expect is that when they achieve their initial objectives, they find they want something more and so the journey continues. The scarecrow, the tin man, the cowardly lion, and even the wizard found that what they thought would be the end point was really a new beginning.

What we need to make the journey is focused on the individual making the trip. Each person requires certain structures and supports to keep them moving forward, whether that is a brain, a heart, courage, or a hot air balloon. In the business journey, there are typical supports, such as expectations, training, time lines, supervision, enticements, and rewards that keep us on the path to success (i.e. the yellow brick road for the travelers to Oz). Dynamics in the workplace, particularly multigenerational workplaces, may require interface, interpersonal discovery, appreciation of the value of difference, and collaboration to achieve a collective goal. There are individual characteristics that play a role in reaching objectives, such as self-discipline, flexibility, creativity, open-mindedness, and determination. Just as each person brings unique abilities to a journey, each comes with unique challenges as well. Fire, water, and fear of inadequacy were individual concerns for our traveling heroes.

The audience includes those invested in a worker's performance. The client, management, supervisor, coworker, mentor, mentee, or anyone impacted by an employee's journey. In our study of generational differences, we have illustrated how individuals can either contribute to or hinder the experience of others. A millennial working on a project for a baby boomer client benefits from understanding the mentality of the baby boomer in producing a successful outcome. Notice the reference to "understanding" the values and expectations of someone from a different generation. A successful workplace journey neither requires nor benefits from every participant becoming like the others. The benefit is in appreciating the difference of perspective and learning how differences help us to expand our perception. The wizard didn't need to become a scarecrow, tin man, cowardly lion, or displaced girl to understand what each was looking for. It was his understanding of their character from listening to their story that enabled him to determine what each needed to achieve their potential.

Challenges and obstacles are a meaningful part of any journey. As authors, the challenge we seek to address is that individuals in the workplace see generational differences as an opportunity rather than a barrier. When we expect complications on the workplace journey, it keeps us mindful of the potential for setbacks, disappointments, and unexpected disruptions on the road to success. Some challenges may be obvious like unrealistic time lines, personality conflicts, or lack of resources. Others will catch us off guard such as a personal crisis or sudden change in personnel. Accepting that there will be potholes in the road helps us stay alert to where we are going and believe that we can find a way around obstacles to achieve a successful end. Thank goodness for the ruby slippers. "Don't be discouraged. Just close your eyes, tap your heels three times, and say 'there's no place like home.'"

Were you surprised by the steps to of becoming a self-leader in the workplace? Probably not since the process is fairly basic. Did you recognize that these steps are the same for individuals from any generation? As has been discussed, there are far more similarities between individuals raised in different time periods than there are differences. Did you notice that the process is the same for the leader of a group as it is for guiding our individual journey? In fact, the greater a leader understands the course planned out by individual team members they are leading, the more effective they can be at developing group collaboration. Can you envision using this process in helping to lay the foundation for success for the next generation?

Workplace success results when self-directed employees have their assets effectively joined with others to collaborate in the achievement of a goal. In the modern workplace, employees raised with different generational experiences are brought together to benefit from their collective abilities in achieving change. When something "Wontwerk," we seek to fix it or have it fixed. When what normally works to fix it doesn't help, we seek creative alternatives, drawing on the value of past experience in combination with fresh, untried ideas. This is the value that results from blending the perspectives of different generations.

Change is not an option; it is a certainty. The option is to embrace change or futilely attempt to resist it. If you doubt the futile aspect, try to keep the weather from happening. In the workplace, every individual has the option to be a learner or a leader, and generational background is not a factor in the equation. Embrace the change; get comfortable with it and enjoy it. It will make your life and the lives of everyone around you better.

Epilogue

Remember our fictitious company "The Old Grande Advertising Agency"?
Even they can achieve harmony and productivity among generations if they
open their minds to what can be. We end with this story that blends reality
and fiction. Who remembers "Who Framed Roger Rabbit"?

I returned to my office that morning in November 2018 after delivering an executive leadership session with a client. They were having a challenge enacting change management in their business. Turnover with newly on-boarded talent was killing their bottom line. They knew that they needed to do something different but weren't sure what that was. The CEO was a friend of one of my Rotary Club members. She had set up the introduction. During my initial presentation, they agreed with the concepts I introduced and appeared to be enthused about what I could do to help them. Now, three sessions into working with them, there were still a couple of top people at Simpson, Evans & Crumb who were reluctant to open their minds to change.

As I got out of my car at my office, I was reflecting on how the entire culture of businesses changes in a positive way when the C-suite people truly get on board. Sure, Simpson, Evans & Crumb liked the concepts that I was helping them implement, but actually changing was still hard. We were making progress slowly and getting some good things in place. The leadership there was mostly baby boomers and older Gen Xers. Getting them to understand that investing in your employees is a good thing proved a challenge. They had yet to realize that businesses that make that happen can actually turn their human resources into human assets. Sometimes people only change when the pain of not changing exceeds the pain of changing. I hoped it wouldn't take getting to that point before we got the whole business on board.

I dropped my bag in the chair by the door and headed around my desk to pick up messages. I stopped to grab a cup of coffee along the way. I settled into my chair and brought my computer back to life. The hot coffee felt good. I could feel its warmth taking the chill away. The first three emails were pretty routine—people wanting me to use their services, a follow up from a previous client, and an industry news message. It was the fourth e-mail, however, that caught my attention. It was from a firm I had not heard of. It read like this:

Good morning, Mr. Butler.

My name is Mina Peasencues. You don't know me, but we have a mutual friend, Marilyn Bannister. Marilyn told me that you were able to help with staffing issues at her company. I am the business development manager and program manager at the Old Grande Advertising Agency. We are a fifty-five-year-old agency that has always been very successful. Up to now, that is. Lately we have been having trouble keeping these young kids focused on their work. They are impossible to work with. I can't understand how they can even keep a job. They only stay with us for a short time, and they don't care to do the work we give them while they are here. It is beginning to affect our ability to hire talent in the first place. Can you help us? If we don't do something soon, we are going to have to close up shop. I would love to talk with you. I can be reached at xxx-xxx-xxxx.

I look forward to hearing from you.

Always,

Mina Peasencues

I chuckled because her salutation reminded me of the old saying, "Always mind your P's and Q's." At the same time, I was intrigued. There was a sense of desperation in Mina's tone that scared me. But that same sense of desperation made me want to find out more. I picked up my phone and dialed her number. She answered on the second ring.

"This is Mina."

"Hello, Mina, this is David Butler with WTG Talent Solutions. I just read your email. Sounds like you have quite a dilemma with your younger talent. A lot of businesses I work with feel that way at first. People from all generations have misconceptions about people in other generations. It creates a lot of conflict in the workplace where there really should be harmony. Helping businesses understand that is what we do best. How do you think I can help you?"

"Thanks for getting in touch so quickly, Mr. Butler. I am kind of stuck in the middle at my office. I am responsible for bringing in new work and getting our current workload out on time. Our CEO, Wyatt Wontwerk, is a stickler for procedures. He inherited the agency from his dad who started it in the early '60s. He runs it the way he learned from his dad. On the other hand, most of the graphic artists are just out of art school. They just don't see why we have to do things the way we always have. I understand where they are coming from and know that they produce great work, but I am stuck in the middle between them and Mr. Wontwerk. If we don't do something soon, there won't be anything left of Old Grande Ad. We need you to help us make it through. Can we meet so I can give you more details?"

I wasn't really in a place where I needed to take on a new client, but something in Mina's voice made me want to help. I took another gulp of my coffee and a deep breath. Old Grande Ad was local so there wouldn't be a lot of travel involved. They also weren't a mega-firm so we could make some real change happen there if we could get the leadership on board. And, my work with Rodgers & Williams, LLC, was winding down. "OK, Mina," I finally said. "I think I have a space coming open in my workload. I am willing to come by your office and take a look at things. No promises that I will take this on, but I will check it out."

"Thank you so much," Mina said. "Tell me what fits your schedule and I will adjust my calendar to make it happen."

"How does next Tuesday morning at 10:00 work for you?"

"Perfect! I have a networking meeting that morning, but I can rearrange to be at the office with you."

"Great!" I replied. "I will add it to my calendar. I know generally where you are, but will you please email me your office address?"

"I will do that right now. Thank you so much for considering this. You have a reputation for being able to make people change. I can't wait to talk more."

"You are very kind, Mina, but there's one thing you need to understand. I don't make people change. I only show them the value in wanting to change and provide some simple ideas of how to bring people of all generations together to create a harmonious workplace. In the end, the people at your business have to want to change. Let's see how we can help you with that first."

I arrived at their ten minutes early. I'm one of those people who think that anything less than five minutes early is considered late. Besides, you never know how long you might get stuck in traffic in the Nashville area. Better to allow a little extra time. I looked around and tried to get a feel of the business. The outside of the three-story building was clean and sharp. They obviously had a decent business if they could afford to work in an office building like this. At two minutes until 10:00 I walked up to the front door and went in. I scanned the board in the lobby and saw that the Old Grande Advertising Agency was on the second floor. I pushed the up button for the elevator and waited. When the doors opened, I saw that their office was directly across the hall. I shook my coat up around my shoulders and went in. The first thing I noticed was that there wasn't a receptionist. That was strange for a business with this outer appearance. After just a minute, a woman came down the hall to greet me. I judged her to be a Gen Xer.

"Mr. Butler," she greeted me. "I am Mina Peasencues. Thank you again for coming to talk with us. I am sorry about not having a receptionist. Ours quit yesterday. She didn't like that Mr. Wontwerk told her that she wasn't allowed to have her phone out at the desk. See, this is what I was telling you about. I am just about at wits' end. Again, thanks for coming. Let's go down to the conference room to talk."

I listened to Mina's story about her three talented but young graphic artists. I could feel her frustration mount as she talked about Wyatt Wontwerk's solutions to managing them. It was pretty easy to see that she was just about at the end of her rope. We talked for about thirty minutes. I made a lot of notes. Much of what was happening among the generations at their business was transparent. She asked me if I would like to meet Mr. Wontwerk. I was anxious to do that. I had a mental image of him from how she spoke of him. I wanted to see if my initial perception was correct. Mina walked down the hall to get him.

Wyatt Wontwerk was much like I expected him to be, yet in some ways very different. I had pictured him as a crotchety old man; much like Ebenezer Scrooge from the way she told me he treated the younger people. In reality, he looked much younger than his age. But, when he began to talk about how impossible "these kids" are to work with, his age started to show. If I decided to take Old Grande Ad on as a client, Wyatt would need to be my project. We ended the meeting in an hour. When we wrapped up, Mina thanked me once again for coming. I told her that I would review my notes and if I decided to work with them would send her a proposal. The ride back home was filled with thoughts.

I realized that if I was going to be able to show them how their culture needed to change in order to make Old Grande Ad a best place to work for all generations, we would need to focus on three areas:

1. **Communication.** Like a lot of businesses, this was the key area for positive change. They talked to each other, but the message sent seldom equaled the message received. We would need to help everyone understand that people preferred to communicate in different ways and making an effort to communicate the way others better received the message was both easy and effective.

2. **Flexibility.** The generational talent they needed to make their business thrive had a different view of how the workplace should be structured. Getting the leadership to see that would be a tough nut to crack. I needed to help them see that the emphasis with everyone, regardless of title, needed to be on results, productivity, and great customer relationships. How you get there is not as important as where you wind up. Strict structure in the new workplace was often an unnecessary hindrance to that. Giving people the freedom to manage their work in the way that works best for them actually sets the stage for increased productivity, accountability, and results.

3. **Cross-mentoring.** After learning how to communicate with each other, their next step needed to be getting generations communicating with a purpose. Understanding that "everyone is a teacher, and everyone is a learner" would be integral to keeping the workplace harmonious.

I also realized that I needed to help them understand some of the basic principles of human interaction. I knew that Wyatt Wontwerk would be the key to making things happen, not only because he was the principle decision maker, but because he was the one who was most stuck in generational thinking. I knew from experience that while most people believed in what I had to say, getting them to spend money to actually make changes in their business was another story. Wyatt would be no different. I would need to make him understand that he would actually be investing in his business. My proposal had two options:

1. I could educate them on the principles of bringing generations together in the three key areas I defined and assist them with implementation. I easily saw from my first meeting with Mina that changing the culture at Old Grande Ad would not be easy. Wyatt liked the way things ran there.
2. I could lead the implementation of the three key areas. I would personally facilitate the focus groups to get a baseline of the current state of people's feelings about their work environment, devise an implementation plan based on that learning, and help all of the leaders get comfortable with the new environment. I knew that this had a better change of "sticking" and make Old Grande Ad a better place for everyone to perform. Once again, getting Wyatt onboard would be the key.

I had Mina set up a meeting for me to meet with her and Wyatt to review the proposal. I was confident that I could show Wyatt how the money he spent with me would forever change his business in a positive way. I helped him see that everyone, regardless of generation, needed the same things in their workplace: community, the feeling that their voice is heard, a place where they could learn and grow, and a motivation that works for them. I showed him how workplaces have far less human resource problems when everyone listens with the intent to understand each other. Learning how to be flexible was the key. I provided him with case study information of how other businesses the size of his saw a return on their investment when they changed their culture. Fortunately, Mina was already on board and was able to help Wyatt with his decision. They chose option two. We were ready to start making Old Grande Ad a harmonious and productive workplace.

The discovery part of getting things in place went well. Most of Old Grande Ad's production team was made up of younger generation people. Most of their leadership team was older. Both groups came in with set ideas about how they wanted the business to be structured. Most of them also wanted to work in a place that met their social needs as well. Showing them that this was possible through listening, understanding, and flexing would be my mission.

I started with Wyatt. We met together several times, and in each session I helped him see that there was little value in being a strict enforcer of his own personal values. We talked about the expense to his business through lost productivity and attrition. Mina was there to reinforce what I shared with him. Eventually he came around and agreed to be open-minded and be the driver of the changes. Mina was elated. She knew that less people challenges would allow her more time to do her real work. With these two key leaders setting the pace, the rest was relatively easy.

Old Grande Ad changed into a workplace that had the reputation of being a best place to work for people of all generations. Productivity rose and attrition dropped. The millennial graphic artists were soon recommending Old Grande Ad to others. They even started bragging that Old Grande Ad was now the "New Grande Ad." Mina now spent her time bringing on new accounts instead of putting out fires among the people. Her doctor told her that she no longer needed her blood pressure medication. Wyatt changed his focus to why it would work instead of why it wouldn't work. He created a new role of chief harmony officer and promoted one of his younger people into that position. Their job was to keep discovering new ideas that would make the culture even more close-knit. Old Grande Ad was making more money than ever.

Wyatt eventually turned the daily operation over to Mina and spent most of his time on his boat. Mina became an advocate for the new-world workplace and was frequently asked to speak on how they changed the culture at the Old Grande Advertising agency. The graphic arts team regularly received Clio Awards for their creativity in advertising. The business thrived.

As I reflected on my experience at the Old Grande Advertising agency, I realized how my new friends there were like the characters from Oz. Wyatt was like the wizard, one who truly wanted to do good things but felt compelled to hide behind the mask of his own personal comfort zone. Mina was just like Dorothy, full of ambition and willing to do whatever was necessary to reach her end goal. She just struggled with what that road looked like and allowed pitfalls along the way to get her off track. The young graphic artists were like the tin man, cowardly lion, and scarecrow. Each of them had a personal need that took precedence in how they approached the road ahead. All of them had to come to the realization that although they were different, they had the same needs. Only then did they begin to come together as a real team. When they were given the space to self-manage, and each took accountability for that, they became unstoppable.

As for me, I felt a great sense of accomplishment in helping enact the change. My motto had long been "The only thing that matters is people; everything else is just stuff." Old Grande Ad was a prime example of how when you put people first, everything else falls into place. I was proud of what they did there. But it was about them, not me; they all did the hard work.

And . . .

They all lived harmoniously and productively ever after.

About the Authors

David Butler has spent his entire career leading teams. He has extensive experience in sales, customer service, manufacturing, learning and development and executive coaching. David learned early on that being a team player is far more important than being an individual contributor. In 2017, he retired from the corporate world to follow his dream of developing leaders to empower teams. He is the founder and principle at WTG Talent Solutions, LLC, and lives by the philosophy that "leaders need people more than people need leaders". David is passionate about helping businesses create a positive workplace. He sees generational dysfunction in business today as "the new frontier of inclusion" and has devoted himself to guiding others on cultivating a dynamic multi-generational workplace where the culture is a hub of harmony and productivity. David is a notable public speaker and leadership coach available to speak in a variety of platforms from keynote presentations to business generational inclusion workshops. He resides in Franklin, Tennessee with his wife and their cat, Shadow and can be reached at www.wtgtalentsolutions.com or 615.500.4719.

Keith Neuber is President and lead trainer for I K.A.N. Presentations. Keith holds a Master's Degree in Clinical Psychology from Eastern Kentucky University.

Keith has worked in the human service field for 45 years as a child and family therapist, clinical supervisor, agency director, employee assistance coordinator and as a trainer and motivational speaker.

Keith provides keynote presentations and lectures nationally for human service providers, business and industry and the general public. In addition to his training and consulting work, Keith serves as CEO for Kreative Kids Learning Center, a large not-for-profit early childhood education provider in the greater St. Louis area. Keith's training motto is . . . "If you're not learning and having fun, then he's doing it wrong."